A ROLL OF
THE DICE

A MEMOIR OF A HUNGARIAN SURVIVOR

By
Agnes M. Schwartz

PublishAmerica
Baltimore

First printing

PublishAmerica has allowed this work to remain exactly as the author intended, verbatim, without editorial input.

Softcover 9781462637263
PUBLISHED BY PUBLISHAMERICA, LLLP
www.publishamerica.com
Baltimore

Printed in the United States of America

My appreciation goes to the
Niles Township Administration
whose grant helped make
this publication possible

Gratitude for editing goes to:

Grassfield Writers' Collective
Betsy Bowse
Tom Kuhn
Mary Sass
Sheila Simon
Roberta Stein

Kudos to Matthew Sackel
For his assistance in bringing this project to fruition

My dearest grandchildren, Charles, Jonathan, Adam and Ashley, you are the catalysts for writing my memoir. Without your encouragement and prodding, my story would have never been told. I dedicate this book to you, to my children, Steve, Bill and Cheryl, as well as to all future generations.

TABLE OF CONTENTS

SECTION TWO

MY CHILDREN, MY DIAMONDS

SECTION THREE
HEARTACHES

SECTION FOUR
GRANDCHILDREN ARE A BLESSING

SECTION FIVE
HENRY

SCAPEGOATS AGAIN

By: Eva Gross

Hitler never died.
He only slumbers.

If in any generation
At some part of the globe
A nation sinks into a slump,

Those with the loudest voice
Search for a scapegoat.

Hitler awakens.

Wearing a different suit,
Shouting in a different language,
But carries the same message of hate.

Camouflage their shortcomings,
The people are pleased to follow him.

PREFACE

I started writing this memoir when I turned sixty in 1993. While I had contemplated doing this for a long time, I suddenly felt an urgency to do so. As each year flew by faster than the previous, I became more and more aware of my mortality. To put my life's story on paper has become increasingly important, important enough to invest in a laptop computer because I knew without that, this project would not get done.

Since I started my story sixteen years ago, I have gone through many computers. After I completed a considerable portion, something happened to me emotionally and I was unable to continue. I gave myself various excuses, none with any validity. My family, particularly you, my grandchildren, got after me and pushed me to finish it for your sake.

The summer of 2009, I finally made this project a high priority while my mind was still relatively clear and active. Since that time, I have worked on my memoir steadily. I didn't realize how much fine-tuning such a story entailed.

Some may consider me to be a person without strong religious beliefs. If one is deemed to be a good Jew because she attends temple regularly and follows all the old Jewish customs, then I guess I am not religious. However, I do have very strong feelings and empathy for my people and value my Jewish heritage.

Jonathan, Adam and Ashley, you came into this world as a result of a mixed marriage, meaning that your dad is Christian and your mother is Jewish, while you, Charles, were born to Jewish parents. According to the Old Testament of the Bible, a child's religion is determined by the religion of the mother. Therefore, whether or not you choose to be observant Jews, you are all Jewish. You have a wonderful, rich heritage. Although Jews make up a small percentage of the world population, for centuries we have been known and envied for being exceptionally bright, ambitious, hard-working professionals and business people. The envy of our capabilities has caused our ancestors a great deal of grief and pain throughout history. The persecution and discrimination against Jews by others is called anti-Semitism.

All of you are now adults. Whether you will live your lives as Jews or Christians is your choice. What I would like to impart to you is a feeling for your ancestors and a love and caring for the State of Israel where Jews from all over the world continue to immigrate to escape tyranny and persecution.

I wish that we, the people of this world, could all consider each other as the children of one God and not as Jews, Catholics, Lutherans, Protestants, Muslims or any other religious sect. What a great world it could be if we were unable to discriminate against each other on the basis of our religious beliefs or because of the color of our skin. People might just run out of excuses for waging wars.

I particularly want to tell you about the horrors of the Nazi era and its far-reaching effects on my life and the lives of all Holocaust survivors. I also hope that putting my past in writing will help authenticate the existence of the Holocaust. Almost sixty-five years after the war ended, I still experience nightmares where I try to hide my children from the Nazis. However, the main reason I feel compelled to write my autobiography is that when my generation is gone, and the cynics will tell you there was no Holocaust, you, my grandchildren, will know, **and I ask that you let the world know**, that indeed it did exist. Hopefully, your generation will become the conscience of the world and will **never allow another Holocaust to happen again**. You must never let the world forget that six million Jews, whose only sin was being Jewish, were slaughtered in the greatest inhumanity of mankind. Teach this to your children and ask them to teach it to their children and grandchildren so the Holocaust will never be forgotten.

Through the years, I have worked very hard at blocking out these terrible memories, but I really have not succeeded. I have made it a point to avoid movies or books that deal with the Nazi era. Some survivors, like Simon Wiesenthal, have dealt with their past by devoting their lives to hunting down and bringing to justice former Nazi officers who perpetrated horrendous crimes against our people. These brave survivors have taken it upon themselves to constantly remind and educate the public about the evils of anti-Semitism. Others, like me, have tried to bury the bad memories of the Holocaust. However, after many years of hiding from it, I learned that I had to come to terms with my past in order to go forward with my life.

The first time I opened up about my childhood was in Florida at your school, Jonathan. You asked me to come and talk to your class. I was totally taken by surprise and didn't know whether I would be able to do so. The reaction of your classmates opened the floodgates to decades of pent-up emotions. Adam and Ashley, I also spoke to your classes. Subsequently, as you all know, I became very involved with the Illinois Holocaust Museum and Education Center. I tell my story to many junior high and high school youngsters. Each year, there are fewer survivors. I truly feel it is incumbent upon us survivors to speak up while we are still able. Meeting a Holocaust survivor makes a much greater impact on youngsters than just looking at World War II artifacts.

Compared to the majority, I was one of the more fortunate survivors. At times, when my life has not gone the way I would have preferred, I have felt guilty for having survived. I rationalize that if God granted me the privilege of living while so many others perished, then I should have done better with my life.

When your parents, my children, were youngsters, my prayer was that I might live long enough to see them grow up so they would not be without a mother as I was. My prayers were answered. I had the good fortune not only to see my children grow up, but even my grandchildren. It has been a delight to watch all of you become honest, caring, successful adults. I am so very proud of all four of you! The possibility of dancing at one of your weddings becomes more real each day.

Charles, I am grateful to you and your wife Angela, for blessing me with Caden, my first great grandchild. May he fill your lives with joy.

No matter what the future holds for me, it is much more than my mother had, who perished in her mid-forties when I was about eleven years old.

I was especially moved the first time I took you, Charles, to Florida and I had all four of my grandchildren together. What a blessing! I also remember December 1994 when my children surprised me with a family reunion at Cheryl's house in Orlando. It was the first time in many years my family came together. That was the best gift I could have ever received, an occasion I will always remember and cherish.

So, with this brief introduction, let's start at the beginning.

SECTION ONE
GOOD TIMES, BAD TIMES

CHAPTER I
EARLY DAYS, HAPPY DAYS

Many years ago Charles Dickens wrote, "It was the best of times, it was the worst of times." That quote sums up my childhood very well. For my parents, Jenő (Eugene) and Margit Grűner, nee Friedmann, 1933 was a very good year. They had a happy marriage, a successful business, and after eight years of marriage, they were expecting their first child. I was born on July 24, 1933 in Budapest, the capital of Hungary.

My paternal grandmother died about a week after my birth. I knew her only through the large portrait that hung above my parents' bed. Supposedly, her last words were: "Take good care of the baby."

My father often told me that he gave the doctor who delivered me an extra $100 when he heard he had a girl. True or not, who cares? The story always made me feel good. Mom and Dad worked together in their store selling yard goods, accessories and novelties to tailors for custom-made suits.

My father was a tall, slim, handsome man, always impeccably dressed. He walked so erectly, he looked like he swallowed a broomstick. He went to the barber for his daily shave and on Sunday the barber came to our apartment to shave him. Dad's pet name for me was "nyuszikám," which translates into "my little bunny." He was a hard worker who lived for his family.

Sunday mornings were our special times. Dad took me either to the park or to visit his family, which consisted of a couple of elderly aunts and a cousin. My mother dressed me in my Sunday best. Depending on the season, it might have been a dark velvet dress hand embroidered with pastel stitching or a frilly organza dress with a big bow in the back. She combed my hair to her satisfaction before she turned me over to Dad for our outing.

Mother was a petite brunette. She was the best mom in the world. She was also a businesswoman and worked with my dad in our store. She, too, was always immaculately dressed. The tailors, my parents' customers, created custom tailored, made to measure suits for Mom and

Dad. Mom's shoes, purse, hat and gloves matched each outfit. Both my parents always looked like they just stepped out of a fashion magazine.

There was always an abundance of love in our home. I don't ever recall a harsh word between Mom and Dad.

Roza and Adolf Friedmann, my maternal grandparents, doted on me. Grandma's salt and pepper hair cascaded to her waist when she combed it out. During the day, she twisted it into a bun and pinned it up at the back of her head. She was short and round, the typical grandmother of yesteryear who spent most of her time in the kitchen cooking and baking delicacies, such as roast duck, fried chicken, palacsinta (crêpes) and apple strudel. She always made time to read me a story and answer my endless questions. *Uncle Tom's Cabin* was one of my favorite books.

Grandpa was tall and wiry. Some of his teeth were missing, and the rest were tobacco stained from his beloved cigars. He knew how to turn my tears to laughter and loved to tell stories of my mother's childhood as I cuddled in his lap.

While Grandma and Grandpa had four grandchildren, I was the only one in Europe. Mother had three sisters: Etta and Betsy in the United States and Elza, the eldest, in Budapest. As a young child, I only knew Etta, Betsy and their families from stories and photographs. Elza and her husband were childless. Elza was a second mother to me. Undoubtedly, she lavished all the love and affection she would have given her own child on me. When adults gathered to play cards or socialize, Elza and I had a "tea party" with my dolls. Her mentoring and love played a large role in my life.

Elza, a very accomplished seamstress, made all my clothes. My friends' mothers often asked where I got my dresses. Elza was married to Kalmár Karchi, an electrician, whose penchant for "pálinka" (liquor) kept him from making a decent living. I don't think it was a very happy marriage, certainly nothing like my parents had. Their home was behind the little electrical shop they operated. It was tiny and dark with hardly any room to sit. They never entertained.

My parents and I lived in a third-floor apartment at Liszt Ferenc Tér 9 (Franz Liszt Park), adjacent to the Liszt Ferenc Zene Akadémia (Music Academy). This academy was probably equivalent to Juilliard in the United States. Mom's youngest sister Betsy was a graduate of that school. We lived in an upscale apartment, though we had no central heating and no hot running water. Our source of heat was a large woodburning stove made of ceramic tiles, situated in the corner of a centrally located room. A small boiler in the bathroom, stoked with coal, provided hot water for our weekly bath and shampoo. Otherwise, each morning we washed to the waist with cold water. It was an eye opener. My mother stood in front of the big ceramic stove holding my clothes near the heat to get the chill out before dressing me.

We cooked and baked on a woodburning stove, but we did have the luxury of two gas burners. Our iron was heated on the stove, as well as the curling iron my mother used in order to make Shirley Temple curls out of my otherwise straight, stringy hair. Mother was a real artist when it came to my hairdo. Thank goodness she only practiced her craft on special occasions as my patience always ran out and tempers flared before she was satisfied with her creation. My coiffure was not complete without a large bow.

Grandma and Grandpa resided in the country (Rákosliget), about an hour's train ride from Budapest. They lived in a little bungalow surrounded by a big yard filled with flowers, fruits and vegetables. They raised chickens, geese and ducks. Grandma sat on the geese and ducks and stuffed feed down their throat to properly fatten them. The fattened geese produced large livers. Roasted, they were a true Hungarian delicacy. The rendered fat from geese and ducks provided a delicious spread for bread and grease for cooking. It tasted heavenly with the dill pickles Grandma put up in big jars and set out in the sunshine to ripen. There was no shortening or cooking oil. We didn't know and didn't care about cholesterol in those days. The fruit trees were heavily laden with delicious peaches and plums; their weight bent the branches to the ground and filled the yard with a delicious aroma. Raspberry bushes lined the back fence. Unfortunately, I was allergic to raspberries. Although I loved them, when I ate them, I broke out in itchy, red hives.

During the summer, I spent several weeks with my grandparents, away from the steamy, bustling city. I slept in a big comfortable bed in a room of my own. The crowing of the roosters, the serenading of the birds and the early morning sun streaming into the room served as nature's alarm clock. Mom and Dad always spent the weekend with us. Elza and her husband often joined them. Grandma outdid herself to feed her family. We all sat around the oval dining room table and shared a sumptuous meal of roast goose, potatoes and vegetables from the garden. Of course, there was strudel for dessert. There was no air conditioning and there were no screens on the windows. The yellow flypaper hung from the dining room light fixture, swinging in the breeze, catching flies, mosquitoes and other flying insects. Grandpa made me a spritzer of wine and soda water to enjoy with my meal. These were wonderful, happy, carefree times.

Even though there was running cold water at Grandma's house, there was still an outhouse next to the chicken coop. My friend Judy, who lived across the street, often came to play with me. During one of her visits, she used the bathroom. Later, Grandpa said: "Next time Judy has to use the bathroom, let her go to the outhouse. It costs too much money to flush the toilet."

Before they retired, Grandma and Grandpa had a shoe store. Grandpa was a shoemaker. I don't remember their working days. I proudly carried the sturdy brown leather backpack he crafted especially for me. When it was filled with books, the weight made me stand erect and tall.

Lavish resorts surround Lake Balaton, one of Hungary's premier vacation spots. Mother and I spent a few weeks each summer enjoying the lake with its sandy beaches and the amenities the resort offered; Dad joined us on the weekends. During the winter, we vacationed at Kékes, a mountain ski resort where I learned to ice skate. My parents never allowed me to ski; they felt it was too dangerous. The food at this resort was delicious. I particularly loved the "caszino tojás," a hardboiled egg with hollandaise sauce. I never heard the phrase, "We can't afford it."

Margit Sziget (Margaret Island) lay in the Danube like a floating floral pillow, separating Buda and Pest. The island, a luscious green spot during the summer, was one of my favorite playgrounds. The "Fedet Uszoda," was a huge complex of swimming pools with a built-in tunnel that allowed swimmers to escape from the heavy smell of chlorine of the indoor pool to the fresh air of the outdoor pool. That's is where I learned to swim. The trainer held a pole like a fishing rod attached to a rope that connected to a halter under my arms. He kept me afloat while I learned the movements of the breaststroke. The final lesson required that I jump into the deep end and then a swim the length of the pool. When the trainer saw I was hesitant, he gave me a friendly shove. By the time I realized what was happening, I had bounced back up to the surface. With a broad grin and a sense of accomplishment, I met this requirement and my lessons came to a conclusion. Ever since, I've had a continuing love affair with swimming and water sports.

Sundays in the spring and fall were spent with family and friends. We either packed a big picnic lunch or went to one of the quaint little inns on the hillside of Buda. We rode a train that climbed the mountainside inching along like a worm to the top. The gears built into the ground engaged the gears under the train as they moved it and its passengers up the mountain. The view overlooking the Danube with its renowned bridges was breathtaking. Sometimes when Dad and I went alone, we rode our bikes. Mom never learned to ride. The inns in the mountains served wonderful home-style cooking, such as chicken paprikás and stuffed cabbage. We dined while the gypsies played their violins for our pleasure and a bit of loose change. Often Elza, Karcsi and my grandparents came along. Hungarians thought nothing of giving children a glass of beer or wine at such outings. I also grew up drinking coffee.

My other favorite playground was the "Város Liget" (City Park), a huge, well-kept park lined with trees and overflowed with colorful, fragrant flowers. The large circular fountain was its focal point. The jets in the center sent water high in the air while smaller jets on the edge spurted water to various levels. I pushed my doll buggy to the park where I always found some other youngsters eager to play hopscotch, jump rope, or hide and seek. The zoo was nearby. An elephant surprised me one day when he reached his trunk out and took my new yellow spring coat right off of my arm. In the same vicinity was the "Angol

Park" (English Park), an amusement complex, with a merry-go-round, roller coaster and other rides.

Like an ice cream vendor in the United States, Város Liget had a milkman who sold individually bottled milk. This milk was not pasteurized, however, and I became deathly ill from it. Much to the relief of my family, after undergoing an extended hospital stay and receiving excellent care from the doctors, I recovered. I must have been very young because I only know about this incident as it was told to me.

I do recall having scarlet fever when I was a preschooler. Those were pre-penicillin days, and scarlet fever was a very serious, contagious illness. The Health Department posted a big red quarantine sign on our door. No one was allowed in or out. It was assumed that I caught scarlet fever from some library books. I believe modern medicine has disproved this theory and determined that direct contact with the germ is necessary in order to be infected. I had a raging fever for many days. My legs were numb and my mother sat for hours on end rubbing them with alcohol. She promised to take me shopping for a new doll when I recovered. She always kept her promise. We named the doll Katy.

As a youngster, I was a very poor eater and a skinny little girl. At age six, before I started school, my tonsils were removed. How I wish they had left them alone. After the operation, my appetite increased and I started to gain weight, which turned into a lifelong struggle. I eagerly awaited the promised ice cream after surgery. Eating ice cream was a rare treat in Europe, but finally when it arrived, my throat hurt too much to swallow it. Ice cream was only available during the summer at specialty stores. It was not sold in groceries or drugstores. Hungary had no American-style drugstores. Apothecaries filled prescriptions. Toothpaste, soap and other over-the-counter items were sold in drugstores.

Since Mom worked, we had a live-in housekeeper, Juliska, whose name as a tot I could not pronounce. I started calling her Gyika. To us, she remained Gyika for the rest of her life. Evidently she loved me very much. Years later, she risked her life to save mine.

As a European child, I took for granted certain luxuries most hardworking Americans never enjoyed. Neither my mother nor I ever lifted a plate, washed a dish, cooked a meal or did any housework. We had a bell at the dinner table that signaled the maid to bring the next course. The table was set with a starched white tablecloth. Matching napkins were rolled and placed in shiny, sterling silver, monogrammed napkin rings. The food was always prepared to perfection from fresh ingredients. There were no canned goods or frozen foods. The main meal of the day, served around 2:00 P.M., consisted of soup, salad, entree and homemade dessert. Chicken paprikás, töltött káposzta (stuffed cabbage cooked with sauerkraut), and Hungarian goulash (beef stew) were some of our favorites. For dessert, we often had noodles or dumplings made out of a potato dough, then boiled and served with a topping of nuts, jelly, or poppy seeds. Sometimes the dumplings were stuffed with plums, then boiled and rolled in breadcrumbs browned in chicken fat. Fancy tortes and cakes were reserved for weekends. Dad either came home for an hour or so to eat, or a messenger boy from the store, on a bike, picked up a well-packed, nourishing hot meal and delivered it to Dad.

* * * * *

As I write about the past, I reminisce. I see a man coming down our street in a horse and buggy. He yells, "Drótos Fótos Tót." People from the surrounding apartment buildings run out with their leaky pots and pans. He repairs the holes by putting a patch on them and makes the cookware usable again. How did he solder or attach the patches without electricity? I also see a young man riding a bike with a large stone spinning wheel sitting on top of the handlebars. He yells, "Kés elezés" and people bring him their knives to sharpen. The annual carnival comes to my street in the spring. The hajó hinta, (a swing shaped like a boat) is located in the parkway right outside my building. I can hardly wait to get into it and go up, up, up towards the sky. There are booths with enticing games. Oh, if I could just win a kewpie doll. But I know that if I don't win it, Elza and Karchi will buy one for me. It was all so long ago, yet it seems like yesterday.

* * * * *

From the time I was old enough to go to school, I always had a German governess. She was supposed to teach me German. The governess usually learned Hungarian before I learned German. After a while I was able to speak it a bit, but never well. German was considered as the universal language of cultured Europeans.

A black lacquered grand piano sat in the living room. My parents wanted to give me a musical education and hoped I might have an aptitude for playing the piano. While I took lessons, my musical knowledge, on a scale of one to ten, remained at zero. I think I was born with lead in my fingers and tin ears because all my piano lessons went for naught. I learned to read music, knew the location of the keys, but the notes I played didn't translate into music. My friend Edith could sing, play the piano, the accordion, the violin or whatever instrument she picked up. My third grade teacher instructed me to lip sync while the class sang. She told me I threw the class off key. I have never forgotten or forgiven her for depriving me of singing along.

Mom and Dad placed tremendous emphasis on my education because very few Jews were admitted to schools of higher learning. Only one percent of a college class could be Jewish. This quota system was known as "Numerus Clausus." Competition was keen. The need to excel was instilled in me from the time I started first grade. Even today I am very conscientious, probably a result of my early childhood training.

The first four years of my schooling were at a Catholic Girls School because it offered the best education in the area. I became well acquainted with the New Testament, part of the daily curriculum. I certainly didn't know at that time that some day this knowledge would play an important part in my survival. There were several Jewish girls in my class. A religion teacher came twice weekly to teach us about Judaism. Hungary was not a democracy; there was no separation of church and state.

When I was born, Hungary was a monarchy; Horthy Miklos was the Regent of the country. Hungarian Catholics constituted approximately 90 percent of the population. The remaining 10 percent were Germans, Slovaks, Croats, Romanians, Jews and Gypsies. The Numerus Clausus law was enacted in 1920, limiting admissions of "political insecure elements" (mostly Jews) to universities. After Word War I, Hungary lost a great deal of territory, and its economy was in a downward spiral. In order to climb out of a depression, it soon aligned itself with Germany and became dependent on the German economy for raw materials and markets. Extreme right wing organizations, like the Arrow Cross Party, increasingly embraced Nazi policies, including those relating to Jews. The government passed the first anti-Jewish law in 1938. This law established a quota system to limit Jewish involvement in the Hungarian economy. In 1938, in light of the Anschluss, the annexation of Austria by Germany, the Hungarian government felt it could not afford to alienate Germany. In the fall of 1938, Hungarian foreign policy became pro-German and pro-Italian. In 1939, the second anti-Jewish law was enacted. This greatly restricted Jewish involvement in the economy, culture, and society. It also significantly defined Jews by race instead of religion. This definition altered the status of those who had formerly converted from Judaism to Christianity. In 1941, Hungary participated in its first military maneuvers as part of the Axis: Germany, Italy and Japan.

We often attended Saturday morning services at the Dohányi Uccai Templom (Dohányi Street Synagogue), one of the most beautiful and also one of the largest temples in Europe. It had three tiers with a seating capacity of 3,000. Built circa 1850 in Gothic-style architecture, it was the first synagogue that housed an organ. It also became the first reformed temple in Hungary.

During the Holocaust, the area surrounding the synagogue became the ghetto. The Nazis decimated the synagogue. They used it as a collection center for Jews before they marched them to the shore of the Danube to be shot into the frigid river. When the Russians liberated the ghetto, they found thousands of corpses scattered inside and outside the synagogue. The mass grave in the courtyard is still visible. During the Communist era, when religion could not be practiced, the synagogue, with its superb acoustic design, became a concert hall. In the 1990s, when the Communist era ended, the synagogue was rebuilt. Movie star Tony Curtis, whose real name was Bernie Schwartz, was of Hungarian descent. He raised several million dollars to rebuild the interior as well as the exterior of the synagogue. A permanent memorial, a weeping willow tree, sculpted by Imre Varga, was erected in its courtyard in 1989. Each leaf bears the name of a victim of the Holocaust. Today's active Jewish community has established an annual Jewish Festival where famous cantors and rabbis from around the world come together and participate.

Grandma and Grandpa Friedmann were Orthodox and kept a kosher home, while my parents, by today's standards, were reformed Jews. Once in a while, however, on the Sabbath when Grandma turned her back, Grandpa would sneak a puff or two on his beloved cigar.

Elementary school in Hungary consisted of four grades. Then, the student progressed either to polgári, a four-year trade school, or to gimnázium an eight-year college-preparatory school. The latter was difficult to get into because of the quota system that kept Jews out of universities. After I finished the fourth grade, my mother and I went to read the list posted on the school's door. The list contained the names of the students accepted into the gimnázium. We eagerly scanned it looking for my name, Grűner Ágnes. There it was! Grűner Ágnes was accepted into the gimnázium. It was a big accomplishment. I am sure my mother appreciated its significance more than I did at that young age.

In 1941 when I was eight years old, I knew virtually nothing about world politics. I was aware that Hungary was a participant in the current war, W.W. II. In school, I was taught that many Hungarian soldiers were dying and they needed warm socks and wrist warmers. I did not know that Hungary and Germany were allies and had no idea that the Germans planned to annihilate the Jews of Europe. I did not understand the various participants in this war. My friend and I wanted to be good citizens and help our soldiers by knitting warm socks. Of course, we didn't know that as Jews, the Hungarian soldiers were our enemies. We needed to buy yarn and knitting needles for our project. However, when we counted our money, we didn't have enough for the necessary supplies. So, during the night, when I presumed everybody was asleep, I reached into my father's wallet and helped myself. I thought no one would ever know what I had done. After all, it was for a good cause.

The following day, my mother confronted me with my misdeed. I was deeply ashamed and very worried about my father's reaction and the dire consequences that would surely follow. Dad came home from work, and I couldn't look him in the eye. I knew I was in big trouble. In a very quiet, somber manner, he asked me: "Did you take some money out of my wallet during the night?"

Sobbing, I said, "Yes, I did. I'm so sorry and I promise I will never, never do it again."

He continued, "Don't you think I know how much money I have in my wallet?" That never even occurred to me! All this happened on the eve of Yom Kippur, the Day of Atonement, the holiest day in the Jewish religion. Jewish law dictates that we not only atone for our sins but also forgive those who had sinned against us. Dad's tone softened as he explained that this was a time to forgive. He wished me a "gut yontev" (a good holiday) and gave me a big hug and kiss. No punishment could have made a greater impact on me. It was a lesson of a lifetime. I never again took anything that didn't belong to me.

It must have been 1941 or 1942, when my mother's two sisters, Etta and Betsy, who had long ago immigrated to Chicago, were finally able to convince my parents that the future for Hungarian Jews was bleak. Until then, Mom and Dad's response always was, "We don't want to leave the rest of the family. We have a well-going business. Jews never had it so good in Hungary."

With the help of Mom's two sisters and their husbands in Chicago, we at last started the immigration process. Huge wicker baskets were packed with our belongings and shipped out ahead of our departure. Unfortunately, we had waited too long. All our papers were in order, but the Germans denied us the necessary visa. We were stuck in Hungary. Our baggage was returned from Lisbon. If the decision to immigrate had been made sooner, my entire life would have been different and my children would have known their maternal grandparents. But this was not meant to be.

Dad was an only child. From his three surnames, I surmise that his mother was married three times. In spite of three marriages, Dad grew up in an orphanage. I've never understood why his mother didn't raise him. Dad not only had three surnames, but they were typically Jewish names: Süskind Grüner Kleinberger. While in our daily lives we only used Grűner, when it came to official documents, all three surnames had to be shown, further complicating our lives.

CHAPTER II
THE HORRORS OF WAR

Time has dulled my memory as to the exact sequence of events. I was old enough, however, to know when my picture-perfect childhood had screeched to a halt. By late 1943, before Germany occupied Hungary, the Nazi movement in Budapest gained momentum. When I walked to school, I had to pass the Arrow Cross (Hungarian Nazi Party) Headquarters. I was constantly reminded by my parents to be sure to walk on the other side of the street and get past that area as quickly as possible. As the Nazi Party's power gained impetus, either our housekeeper or my mother walked me to and from school. The war escalated; bombings by the Allies became more frequent and intense. There was total blackout; after dark, no lights were permitted to shine through the windows. Some food items became scarce. It soon became apparent that after we heard the German code on the shortwave radio, "Achtung, achtung lichtspiele," air raid sirens followed, alerting the public to seek shelter. Most often, the bombings occurred during the night. Hurriedly, we would put on some warm clothes, grab a few necessities, including a flashlight to guide us, and head for the basement. We could hear bombs whistling and exploding while our three-story brick building shook as if there were an earthquake. After each boom, we waited and wondered whether our building had been hit and whether it was about to cave in on us. After we heard the "all clear" siren, we would emerge from the basement. As we walked up the stairs, we would see the inferno illuminating the sky. It seemed like the flames were licking the stars. The air was thick with smoke. Rubble from bombed out buildings surrounded us.

Despite the fact that it was illegal for Jews to own and listen to a shortwave radio, our ears were constantly glued to it. We looked to America's President Roosevelt and pinned all our hopes on him to rescue the Jews of Budapest from the Nazis. While we thought of him as our savior, he was returning shiploads of Jews to Europe to be slaughtered rather than granting them political asylum. After I learned about this, my former hero, President Roosevelt, fell from his pedestal.

The summer of 1942, when I was nine years old, my mother suddenly appeared at Grandma's in Rákosliget, and whisked me back to Budapest. My family and their friends whispered among themselves trying to shield me from the stark reality of the changing times. Instead of going home, Mom and I stayed with friends. In fact, we were hiding at the home of the Pista and Lilli Deutsche, a Jewish family. The Gestapo had arrested my father. At that time they were arresting people suspected of Polish heritage. His multiple surnames always complicated our lives. After several weeks, or so it seems to me, Dad was released and came back to us and we returned to our home on Liszt Ferenc Tér. Our daily activities resumed in a somewhat normal fashion. Mom and Dad returned to work and I went back to school.

In March 1944, the Germans occupied Hungary. Since Hungary and Germany were allies, the occupation went smoothly without any resistance. There was vague news of atrocities, such as deportations to work camps in the outlying areas, but the Jews of Budapest still did not take this seriously. We later learned that 450,000 Jews were deported within fifty-five days from all of Hungary, except Budapest. As a precaution, we moved Grandma and Grandpa from Rákosliget to Budapest. People were still convinced that no deportation could take place in the big city. We had to wear a yellow star when we stepped out of the house. The star had to be sewn on tightly enough that a pencil couldn't be slipped between the stitches. My father lost his business. I could no longer go to school. Nobody realized that the worst was yet to come. Even as a child, I knew fear. Just to walk out of the house was dangerous for a Jew. It was not uncommon for someone to go for groceries and never be seen again. People simply vanished. The good customers from our store were no longer our friends. They were afraid to be associated with a Jewish family.

In June 1944, we had to leave our home and move into a "Jewish designated" multi-story apartment building, only about a block from where we had lived. Our new home had two bedrooms. My parents, grandparents and I lived in one; two strangers, a mother and her daughter, occupied the other. We lived in constant fear, with filth and hunger. Any knock on the door sent chills through everyone. It could be the Gestapo!

According to the law, all bathtubs had to be filled with water to extinguish a possible blaze caused by bombing. It's hard to imagine how a tub of water could extinguish a raging fire. I had come from a pristine home where the parquet floors were polished and the rugs vacuumed each day. Until then, I had never seen a bedbug. Now, they were plentiful. Their bites caused large welts on our bodies. During the night, the two ladies shook their nightgowns into the tub to rid themselves of the bugs. Dead bedbugs, like a blanket, covered the top of the water every morning.

Our lifestyle had surely changed, yet the bedbugs were a minor inconvenience. My mother, a businesswoman, had never even made coffee; she certainly never cooked, but Grandma made do with whatever ingredients she could find. Jews were only allowed to shop for groceries late in the day. By that time, most of the goods were gone from the store's shelves.

While living at the Jewish designated building, Grandpa became ill and we took him to a hospital where I am certain he did not receive any care. The last time I saw him, he was lying on a cot, like in an old war movie, with beds upon beds all in a row. I always thought he died from coronary problems, while Aunt Betsy thought cancer, a result of smoking his beloved cigars, snuffed out his life. Perhaps he was lucky to die in a bed rather than in a gas chamber.

In July 1944, Horthy Miklos (Nicholas Horthy), the Regent of Hungary, ordered a stop to the deportations, giving Hungarian Jews a short respite. By this time, all the Jews of Hungary, except those living in Budapest, had been deported.

In October 1944 Horthy announced that Hungary would surrender and withdraw from the Axis. He was forced to resign, placed under house arrest and was taken to Bavaria. The Hungarian Nazi Party, the Arrow Cross, headed by Ferenc Szálasi, took over the rule of Hungary. This was the turning point for the Jews of Budapest. Deportations resumed on November 8.

On a cold winter morning, a group of storm troopers in their dark uniforms and highly polished boots appeared in the courtyard of our building. A shot into the air got everyone's attention. All residents froze and became silent from the fear of the unknown. We knew it couldn't be good. The Nazis ordered all men between certain ages, probably 18-50, young enough to be productive in a slave labor camp, to line up downstairs. Dad fell into this category. We had no idea where they were taking him.

A few days later, precisely on November 20, 1944, another band of storm troopers appeared. Once again, the now familiar shot rang out into the air. This time they rounded up women of the same age group. Mom had to go, and that was the last time I ever saw her. I was eleven years old. She tried to put on a brave face as she kissed me goodbye. She was herded away at gunpoint, bundled up in her grey Persian lamb coat and high boots with a backpack containing mere necessities. I have photographs taken during the summer of 1943, when I was picnicking and frolicking in the sun. I didn't have a care or worry in the world. The fate of the Jews of Budapest had changed overnight. Once Mom was gone, only Grandma and I remained. We had lost touch with mother's sister Elza and her husband.

A few days after Mom was led away, Dad returned. He explained that he had escaped en route to Germany. Two Nazi officers sought directions to Budapest. Dad spoke German fluently and became their guide. Because of this quirk of fate, he wasn't deported. When he learned Mom had been taken away, he was heartbroken and wanted to go after her. He said, "I know where they took her. They are assembling the people at the brickyard in Óbuda." Brickyards were always located by railroad tracks, enabling the Nazis to herd the Jews into cattle cars. I was terribly scared and I pleaded with him to stay with me. Had he gone, no doubt he would also have been deported. It was impossible for one Jew to help another.

The next significant thing I remember was, once again, a knock on the door. It was Gyika, our former housekeeper. She came to take me home with her to hide me from the Nazis. I loved her and trusted her. I was totally comfortable with her. Grandma and Gyika threw a few articles of clothing into a bag; removed the yellow star from my coat, as we headed for her apartment. That was the last time I saw my darling grandmother. Gyika lived in a fifth floor flat at Semmelweiss Ucca (Street) 15 in Budapest. We created a new identity for me and rehearsed it over and over again. I became her niece, fleeing from the Russians invading eastern Hungary. She taught me the rosary and some other Catholic prayers and customs. My knowledge of the New Testament, acquired at the Catholic school, came in handy. Now I was known as Balázs Ágnes.

Gyika's pantry was well stocked with staples: potatoes, dry beans, and various smoked meats. We had no idea how long this food might have to last. Her neighbor Theresa was a known Nazi sympathizer; it was imperative that she didn't find out my true identity. Had Theresa reported us, we would have been instantly killed. We knew nothing about my family's whereabouts.

Towards the end of November 1944, a few days after Gyika took me home with her, all remaining Jews were herded into the Budapest ghetto. This ghetto was very different from the ghettos in the United States. Barbed wire fences surrounded the Budapest ghetto. Once inside, there was no getting out. People were packed in one on top of the other. There was no food, no medicine, no clean water. As time went by, more and more people in the ghetto died. Their bodies were thrown in a pile in the streets. All this happened during the time I was in hiding at Gyika's home. I never witnessed it. I only found out about the ghetto after the end of the war.

During my stay with Gyika, air raids became more frequent and intense. Bombs virtually rained from the skies around the clock. All residents of our five-story building moved into the basement for shelter. We lived in the damp, dark cellar for a couple of months. There were no toilet facilities; a bucket was passed around. We slept next to each other on blankets placed on a pile of wood, probably chopped for heating the premises. The bombs whistled and exploded with a bang like huge claps of thunder. Fires raged everywhere and the ground trembled as if gripped by the wrath of God, shaking and collapsing brick buildings as if they were made of straw. Fear permeated the air as we wondered what would kill us first, the bombs or the Nazis.

After a while, the bombing slowed and eventually stopped. An occasional round of machine gun fire could still be heard. News reached us that guerilla warfare was taking place in the streets of Budapest. Engaged in hand-to-hand combat with the Nazis, the Russians moved from building to building, liberating people along the way. We began to feel a glimmer of hope.

By December 26, 1944, the Russians had completely surrounded Budapest. On January 18, 1945, the Nazi regime in Pest fell and on February 13 Buda followed.

To some, the Russians were rapists, looters and savages; to me, they were lifesavers. Gyika tried to tell me that if a Russian soldier approached me, I should tell him that I was very young, just a little girl. I had no idea what she was talking about. Word spread that the war was over in our area. We carefully opened the basement door and slowly, like turtles from their shells, stuck our heads out to look around. After being in the dark for a long time, our eyes had to adjust to daylight. Our building was in shambles. The front staircase was missing, but the back stairs were useable. Gyika's apartment was intact.

The devastation was beyond belief. No building was left unscathed. The air reeked of death. It was difficult to breathe the fire and smoke-filled air. Dead bodies as well as horses littered the streets. People were so hungry they were eagerly carving up the dead horses for food. There was no electricity. There were no telephones, no transportation, no means of communication. We had no idea who had lived or died. The war was finally over. We no longer feared for our lives.

It's a miracle that diseases due to lack of sanitation didn't kill us. My hair was full of lice. Gyika used a fine-toothed comb and kerosene to rid me of these pests. Compared to our previous life and death situation, this problem was of secondary importance. We were alive!

CHAPTER III
PICKING UP THE PIECES

There was nothing to do but wait for news to arrive regarding the fate of my family. And then, while playing in the corridor in front of the apartment, I looked up and saw my father walking towards me. I wasn't sure whether or not I was dreaming as I flew into his arms. There were so many unanswered questions. He was skin and bones. The only thing that mattered at the moment was that he was alive.

How did he know where to look for me or how to find me? Did he know that Gyika was the one person he could trust and count on? Was it prearranged between my parents and Gyika that if my life were in jeopardy, she would hide me? Did my dad pay her to hide me? If he did, the reward does not lessen her heroic deed. She risked her life to save mine.

Dad told us a sketchy story of his survival. He had been living in a Swedish protected house. The term, "Swedish protected" means that Sweden guaranteed Germany that when the war was over, Sweden would accept and resettle in Sweden a certain number of Jews. There were some Swiss protected buildings, too. People lived like sardines in a can. There was no food, hardly any air to breathe or space to stretch a leg. No matter how bad the living conditions may have been, they were better than in the concentration camps.

A Swedish diplomat, Raoul Wallenberg, played a major role in saving many Hungarian Jews by providing them with the necessary papers that would admit them into a Swedish protected building. A few decent people still existed in the world. Raoul Wallenberg literally pulled some Jews out of cattle cars headed for Auschwitz. Unfortunately, fate was not very kind to Mr. Wallenberg. The Russians deported him to Siberia and no one knows what happened to him. I would very much like to know whether he was instrumental in saving my dad's life, but there is no one to ask, no one left to answer my questions.

Information about family and friends trickled down slowly. Everybody always whispered around me. They wanted to spare the child from the realities. However, I overheard enough to know that Grandma,

Elza and her husband had been moved into the ghetto. On a cold winter night, they were marched to the shores of the Danube where they were shot into the freezing river and left to die. As ammunition dwindled, the Nazis improvised by wiring several people together before firing one shot. That way, they accomplished their dastardly deed of killing as many as ten people with one bullet. They had become masters at exterminating Jews. Members of The Arrow Cross, the Hungarian Nazi Party, eagerly assisted the Germans in their sadistic act.

In April 2005, a memorial of sixty pairs of cast iron shoes, sculpted by Gyula Pauer, was placed along the shores of the Danube, in memory of the innocents shot into the river. In my eyes, the blood of the Nazis' victims had permanently tainted the once beautiful blue Danube bloody red.

After the Russian occupation, we learned that the ghetto was wired with dynamite, ready to be blown sky high at the blow of a whistle. The ghetto housed the elderly, the infirm and the children. They were of no use to the Germans. Those capable of slave labor already had been deported to the various camps. We still didn't know anything about my mother.

Much later, I learned that Károly Szabó, an employee of the Swedish Embassy in Budapest, arranged a meeting between Raoul Wallenberg and Pál Szalai, a high-ranking member of the Budapest police force and the Arrow Cross Party, in an effort to save the inhabitants of the Budapest ghetto. Wallenberg learned that Adolph Eichmann planned to massacre the remaining residents of the ghetto. The only one who could stop this mass murder was the commander of the German troops in Hungary, General August Schmidthuber. Wallenberg sent Schmidthurber a note promising that he, Wallenberg, would make sure that the general was personally held responsible for the massacre and that he would be hanged as a war criminal at the end of the war. By that time, the German's knew that the end of the war was imminent and the Nazi era was just about over. The bloodbath was halted in the last minute as a result of Wallenberg's daring action.

Soon after our reunion, Dad and I got on a freight train and set out for the country to recuperate. There were no passenger trains running. Like a couple of hobos, we jumped on a freight train; destination unknown. There were many other dazed people on this train, looking for their homes, families and loved ones. We were all in a fog. We needed to get away from the bombed out city to find a place with sufficient food. The train had no toilet facilities. A little potty was passed around as needed and the waste was dumped through the open door. It reminded me of the bucket in the basement. This was no time to worry about privacy.

We got off at a small village; I have no idea of its name or location. There, we rented a room from a farmer. I am still curious where my dad got the money to pay for our little vacation. He needed rest and good food to recuperate.

On the evening of our arrival, our hostess prepared a platter of the most delicious scrambled eggs. It had been years since we'd even seen an egg and it was the best thing we had eaten for a long, long time. We ate with voracious appetites until our stomachs could hold no more. There were chickens, geese, livestock, fruits and vegetables on the farm. The farmer's wife was a good cook and we devoured the meals she prepared. We relaxed and talked in an endeavor to regain our strength and sanity.

Soccer was, and still is, Hungary's national sport. It was Dad's favorite pastime. While on the farm, we attended several local matches. After a few weeks, we moved back into our apartment on Liszt Ferenc Tér. Surprisingly, we found the apartment intact although strangers, a family of three, had occupied it. We shared our two-bedroom apartment with its current residents until they moved to a different home. Unlike most Jews, we found our furniture and belongings where we had left them. Dad's elderly Aunt Mariska, a diabetic, came to live with us. I wonder how she survived. Perhaps the lack of food kept her diabetes under control. Before the war, she had shared an apartment with her sister and nephew. They were now gone. She needed a home and Dad thought it would be good if she kept an eye on me. I never had a close relationship with her, and I was not thrilled with her company. I wanted my mother back! We still had no idea of her whereabouts.

Trainloads of deportees returned daily from Germany. With each group, I awaited my mother but my hopes never became reality. A survivor of the Bergen-Belsen Concentration Camp contacted Dad at his store. She told him that she was with my mother when she died on Friday, January 13, 1945 of so-called natural causes. That meant she was neither shot nor gassed; she was just unable to withstand the horrible living conditions and the typhus that ran rampant in the camp. They must have been very close friends for this woman to remember the exact date my mother died. Anne Frank also lost her life at this camp. In April 1945, the British liberated the Bergen-Belsen camp. If Mom could have just held out for a few more months . . . . but, she was gone, gone forever. In June 1945, the Allies liberated all the camps. I could not believe that Mom would never return and kept hoping each day she would walk through the door. I was convinced her friend was mistaken, that sooner or later, my mother would come back and hold me in her arms again.

The returning refugees brought back unbelievable horror stories about their own fate as well as the fate of their families. They were in deplorable condition, starved and sick. My mother's cousin Erna told us about her children being torn from her arms and sent to the ovens. Men, women and children were separated, entire families destroyed. Had Erna clung to her children, they all would have died in the gas chamber. Perhaps she would have preferred dying with her children to surviving without them. Others told of babies being torn from their mothers' arms and flung against a wall where their brains splattered in front of their mothers. Men and women were marched to the showers, but instead of water, poisonous gas flowed from the showerheads, killing hundreds at a time. Special ovens cremated bodies around the clock. Nazi physicians performed cruel medical experiments on their prisoners. Dr. Josef Mengele, the "Angel of Death," was the most notorious for his cruel experiments, particularly on twins. His white-gloved fingers pointing either to the right or to the left at the new arrivals in Auschwitz determined in an instant who would live or die. Those who had met Dr. Mengele described him as a handsome, charming, soft-spoken man. They never suspected that the devil lurked in his heart and ice water flowed through his veins.

Mom's two cousins, Erna and Lajcsi, returned from the camps, but both lost their spouses and children. Before the war, I had been a flower girl at Lajcsi's wedding. Elza made me a pink silk dress with a shirred bodice and a large velvet bow in the back. I still have a photograph of Elza holding my hand, walking down the steps of the synagogue after the ceremony. Eventually, both Lajcsi and Erna left Hungary. Lajcsi moved to Israel where he remarried and started a new family. Erna joined her mother and brother in Argentina. She also remarried.

Our entire world had gone insane. Many Jews committed suicide rather than wait to be murdered. I am surprised there weren't more. What was the point in living and suffering when each and every Jew was earmarked for death? The world has attempted to destroy Jews from the beginning of time. After each pogrom, enough Jews survive to rebuild their lives and multiply. Is this an accident or God's design?

As soon as it was possible, Dad legally changed our last name from Süskind, Grüner, Kleinberger to Gabányi, which is an unmistakably Hungarian name. Many Hungarian Jews did likewise. Dad got his business back, and I went back to school at the Jewish Girls Gimnázium. A small group of us, friends before hell on earth hit us, reconnected. There was an unspoken code of silence among us. Nobody talked or asked about what happened during the Nazi occupation. Some of my friends lost both parents, while others lost one. Miraculously, the entire family, mother, father and sister of my dear friend Ágnes Fischl survived. Her family immigrated to Palestine, which later became Israel. I find it inconceivable that we did not question what happened to our families; we just accepted it as a matter of fact. Why were we scared to say to each other, "Where is your mom, what happened to your dad?" Today that seems to be such an obvious question.

None of my friends knew I had been in hiding, and I knew nothing about how or where they survived. Had our past left us so fearful that we couldn't ask any questions? Probably so. By the time I wanted to ask questions, there was nobody left to answer them.

The first Passover after we learned of Mom's fate, I put an extra place setting on the table. Dad came home from work and looked at me as if asking, who is coming to dinner? Our eyes met and there was no need to speak. The extra place setting remained unused. No matter how much I wished, I could not bring Mom to the Passover table. When I opened the door for Elijah, I expected Mom to walk in. Dad bought me a gold necklace with a little medallion. My mother's date of death, January 13, 1945, was inscribed on the back. I wore that necklace for years without taking it off. Recently, I gave it to my daughter Cheryl to hold for my only granddaughter until she is old enough to appreciate its significance.

As time passed, the dream of my mother's return dimmed, but it took years for my hope to vanish.

Dad met Hermina, a woman he had known before he married Mom. Her husband had not returned from the camps either. They started to date. Hermina tried her best to win me over by cooking and baking my favorite dishes and buying me trinkets she thought would please me. Nevertheless, I disliked her intensely. In my eyes, she was a trespasser, an intruder on my time with Dad. Besides, I did not want her in the way when Mom returned.

Eventually, Dad and my mother's two sisters in Chicago made contact. Once again, the immigration process to the United States was set in motion. I am deeply grateful that my children were born and grew up in America. While this country may not be perfect, undoubtedly, it is the best place on earth.

Forty-one years after immigrating to America, in March 1988, I was in my mid-fifties on my way to work in Chicago when I experienced a pain in my chest that radiated down my left arm. While the pain was not intense, it was persistent. After getting off the train, I stood on the street corner pondering whether to ignore the discomfort and go to work, or seek medical attention. I looked up, and there was an empty cab before me. It was as if the decision had already been made. I got into the cab and directed the driver to take me to Weiss Memorial Hospital where my doctor was on staff. Seeking medical attention at that time turned out to be crucial in averting a possible massive coronary. I have always believed that Mom's guiding hand made that decision for me. I haven't seen her since I was eleven years old, but her presence is always with me. I have had to make many important decisions by myself. At times of crisis, I have always felt her loving hand pointing me in the right direction, showing the way.

We never forget; our past is always with us. We all deal with grief in our own way, but it never leaves us. I have tried to tuck the bad memories away in the back of my mind, thinking that I have buried them. Then suddenly, when least expected, I wake up screaming from a nightmare that brings back the old terror. I will never forget the sound of the SS soldiers' boots as they hit the pavement. Even their steps, as they walked in cadence in their highly polished, shiny boots reflected their arrogance. Their every step resonated an unforgettably ominous sound.

CHAPTER IV
COMING TO AMERICA

In January 1947, Dad and I left Hungary and headed for the United States. Since our immigration papers had been approved years before, we were among the first to leave after the war and before the Iron Curtain dropped. I was a frightened, naive thirteen year old with heavy emotional baggage.

Gyika saw us off at the railroad station. It had been extremely difficult to say goodbye. We both knew we would never see each other again. Before we parted, she gave me a ring, a memento I will always cherish. When I think of Gyika, I see her caring eyes, a colorful scarf around her head and a gold tooth shining in her mouth. I wish I had her photograph. We corresponded and kept in touch over the years until she died of cancer.

* * * * *

In 1988, I contacted Yad Vashem, the Israeli Holocaust Museum, and requested that Juliska's name be inscribed in the Avenue of the Righteous Christians. This was the only thing I could do to repay her courageous deed. They wanted proof and I had none. All I could do was relate what she did for me. We corresponded back and forth for approximately two years before they granted my request. I was glad to be able to honor her by preserving her name historically.

* * * * *

Dad and I rode a train from Budapest to Berlin. We spent the night in an old bombed-out hotel that didn't look much different from the ruins we left behind in Budapest. I couldn't wait to get out of Germany. The following day we boarded a Pan Am propeller plane. We were on our way to a new life in a better world, the United States. Our optimism dampened when we encountered a storm over the Atlantic. The winds threw the plane around as if it were a paper kite. Everybody aboard vomited and prayed. We made an unscheduled emergency landing in Newfoundland and waited for the weather to clear. They put us up in barracks, men in one room and women in another. I would not leave my father's side and spent the night with him and the other men. Next day, we were ushered into a lovely dining room with white tablecloths. I don't remember the food they served, but I certainly remember the ice cubes in the water glasses. I had never seen an ice cube before. It was a little thing that made a huge impression on me. In Hungary, the iceman delivered ice in big blocks, certainly not in little cubes. In Hungary, nobody ever put ice in a glass of water.

Upon landing in New York, I saw a black man mopping the floor at the airport. I had only seen black people in the movies where they were depicted as cannibals. I was so scared of being eaten alive that I clung to my father with all my might.

My entire world revolved around my dad; the rest of the family I had known and loved from birth was gone. Unfortunately, he had filled my head with some very erroneous ideas about life in America. Whether he truly believed the stories he told, I will never know. He told me I was lucky to be the only girl in the family. My three cousins were boys. Since I was the only girl, I would be the little princess. He said that in the United States, everybody was rich; that people threw dirty clothes in the garbage and replaced them with new ones; that the streets were paved with gold; that milk and honey flowed from the mountains.

Upon our arrival in New York, Uncle Eugene Kuhn, Dad's brother-in-law, met us at the airport and the three of us took the train to Chicago. Before we left New York, we ate lunch at an Automat. There, after depositing some coins, sandwiches were dispensed through a little window. I couldn't believe what I saw.

While riding the train, we had dinner in the dining car. There was a small green fruit on my plate. My uncle asked, "Do you like that?"

I replied, "Oh, I love it."

I spit the fruit out as quickly as I bit into it. In Hungary, Grandma used to pickle small green tomatoes. That's what I thought I was biting into, but it turned out to be an olive. I had never tasted an olive, and it certainly didn't taste like Grandma's pickled tomato.

Although I had taken some English classes in Budapest, I quickly realized that the English I learned in the classroom was very different from the English spoken in the streets. For all practical purposes, I had no conversational skills.

The Kuhn family, Aunt Betsy, Uncle Eugene, and my two cousins, Paul and Tom, lived in an apartment at 6423 North Claremont in Chicago. Upon our arrival, my new American family took a look at me. They expected to see a skinny, starved little girl. Instead, they got a chubby child. Post war, we had received wonderful packages from America, filled with boxes of Hershey bars, home made chocolate chip cookies, powdered eggs, powdered milk and canned goods. Besides the chocolate, I particularly liked the cream of mushroom soup. These were all high calorie items. With my mother and my loving European family gone, food became my emotional crutch.

My father stared at the blue jeans my cousins were wearing. In Budapest, there was no blue denim. That was not elegant enough for the always perfectly dressed Hungarians. He couldn't understand how people could allow their children to walk around in such clothes. He could not have guessed that years later jeans would be fashionable worldwide.

Uncle Eugene, a CPA, was an old fashioned European man who never set foot in the kitchen. Aunt Betsy, my mother's youngest sister, was a typical housewife. Her domain was the kitchen, her main job the rearing of the children. My cousin Paul was a year older than I was, and his brother Tom was two years younger. Paul was quiet and studious, and for the most part, ignored me. Tom and I established a good rapport. In spite of the language barrier, we managed to communicate. He was a Cub Scout, and I stitched his merit badges to his sash. I also sewed an apron for his home mechanics class.

Tom asked me one day, "Do you like ice cream sundaes and sodas?"

I said, "I don't know what you're talking about. I've never heard of a sundae or soda."

He said, "Come on, let's go."

Tom took me to the Stineway Drug Store on the corner of Western and Devon, just a couple of blocks from home. We sat at the fountain. Tom ordered a chocolate sundae and a chocolate soda, and we shared. One was better than the other. I thought I was in heaven as we licked our spoons until there wasn't a drop left.

Dad slept on a daybed in the dining room. The back room, probably used as a den before our arrival, was turned into a bedroom for me. In Europe, I shared a room with my parents. For the first time, I had a room of my own. Tom and I became pals. He would come into my room when everyone thought we were asleep and teach me about America and American customs. When I saw him shivering in his pajamas, I invited him to get under the covers to keep warm. One night, my dad walked in on us and routed Tom from my bed. That put an end to my night classes. Tom was eleven; I was thirteen.

Mother's oldest sister, Ethel (Etta), was married to George (Gyüri) Gaal. They were both physicians. I don't know how or where in Europe she was able to attend medical school to become a doctor. Very few medical schools accepted women, let alone Jewish women. I have been told that when she first came to Chicago, she wrapped soap in a factory until she had sufficient English skills to pass the Medical Board exam and became a licensed physician in the United States. Their son, Peter, was an only child.

In 1929, Aunt Betsy came to the United States to lend a hand to her sister when Etta was expecting a baby after a previous miscarriage. Etta was frail and needed assistance before and after the baby arrived. The Gaals, Gyüri and Etta, belonged to a social club of Hungarian Jews. Uncle Eugene, who arrived in this country in 1922, was also a member. The Gaals took Aunt Betsy to their club to introduce her to their friends. There, she met Uncle Eugene. Other Hungarians had previously told Uncle Eugene about Aunt Etta's attractive sister who would be soon arriving from Budapest. He was immediately captivated by her beauty and charm. Six weeks later, they were engaged, later married and settled in Chicago.

Aunt Etta was very kind and warm hearted. I always enjoyed spending time with her and looked forward to Sundays when I took the streetcar on Western Avenue to visit with her. They had a live-in housekeeper, Mrs. Moore, who did the cooking and cleaning. Unfortunately, Aunt Etta had high blood pressure and the wonder drugs of today did not exist. As a result, she suffered several heart attacks, which made her a semi-invalid and took her to the grave at age 50.

Probably the heartbreak and anxiety of the loss of her family in Europe was a contributing factor to that heart attack.

When I was fourteen, Aunt Etta and Uncle George took me on a motor trip through Canada where I got my first black dress. The taffeta swished with every step I took. The dress had a full circle skirt and a big bow on the bodice. I felt very grown up and elegant in my new dress and my high heeled platform shoes. Another time, they took me to the Chicago Stadium to see a three-ring circus. I was awed by the glitter and dazzle and did not know which way to look first. I had never seen anything like it before. Where I had come from, circuses were held under a tent, one act at a time.

Uncle George, while quite handsome, was not always pleasant. He was a pompous, stuck up womanizer who liked the ladies and flaunted his infidelity. Aunt Etta certainly deserved much better. I have often asked myself why a woman of her stature would put up with a husband who caused so much pain. Eventually, I concluded that divorce at that time was truly frowned upon and the welfare of their only child was paramount.

Aunt Etta was a pioneer in birth control. Her office was in her home. While visiting her, I went to the washroom where I saw several "rubber balls cut in half" around the sink. I was curious and asked what they were. She explained that they were diaphragms used to avoid unwanted pregnancies. That was my introduction to birth control.

When I was sixteen, while away at summer camp, Aunt Etta succumbed to a massive heart attack. Her death caused me great anguish and another loss in my life. I pondered, why do people I love leave me and die? She died on Friday, July 13; my Mother died Friday, January 13, different years, of course. Aunt Betsy had lost her last sister. She was overwhelmed with grief. My cousin Peter, Aunt Etta's only child, was born on July 24. I was also born on July 24, three years later. Isn't it strange that Peter and I were born on the same day and both of our mothers died on Friday, the 13th? To this day, my one and only superstition is that bad things happen on Friday the 13th.

Soon after we arrived in Chicago, Dad was diagnosed with tuberculosis. He was shipped off to Winfield Sanitarium where we visited him every Sunday. The rest of the family immediately underwent chest x-rays to determine if any of us was infected. Several years later when Paul entered medical school, he reacted positively to a TB test, which showed that he had been exposed to the disease, but his immune system had fought it off. I could only talk to Dad through the window; I was not allowed to enter his room. Paul and Tom must have resented spending every Sunday traveling to Winfield, and I can't really blame them. After all, my dad and I were outsiders who intruded upon their lives.

I felt terribly alone. Even though I was with family, they had not been part of my life until now. They were strangers to me. I did not speak their language and instead of being the princess Dad described, I felt like Cinderella before the ball. In Europe, I grew up in a home where I never was asked to do any housework as we always had a live-in housekeeper. Now I had to do the nightly dinner dishes, iron my own clothes, and do other household chores. It was a difficult situation for all of us. Had my upbringing been different during my early years, I would have thought nothing of helping. In fact, I was never asked to do anything that I didn't ask of my own children years later.

After several months at Winfield Sanitarium, Dad was pronounced negative. Since he was no longer contagious, he was discharged. I had waited for such a long time and looked forward to having Dad back with me. However, he had different ideas. He wanted to return to Budapest. Dad reasoned that it was too difficult to learn English and assimilate into a different culture. To this day, I cannot understand how he could have left me alone. I know the war took a toll on him, but how could he leave his only child? He and I were the only survivors; there was no one else left. We needed each other.

I was even more devastated when I found out that my father had sold his business in Budapest with the contingency that if he returned within a year, the business would revert to him. It became clear that he had planned to return to Hungary before we even left. He never really intended to stay with me in the United States. He delivered me to my mother's sisters as if he were UPS dropping off a parcel. Once they accepted delivery, he was finished with me. Having recently lost my mother and being soon thereafter deserted by my father was way too much. I could not understand how he could have abandoned me.

Over the years I have tried to look at the situation from his viewpoint, but I really have never come to terms with it. As a child, I didn't immediately understand that he made me an orphan. Upon Dad's request, Uncle Eugene paid his airfare back to Europe, but refused to pay for my return. I am very grateful to my uncle and aunt for keeping me here and preventing my father from taking me back to a place that had become a large cemetery to me.

Dad felt his American in-laws blamed him for surviving while their sisters and parents perished. There could be some truth to that. On the other hand, it is not unusual for Holocaust survivors to have such guilt feelings. Emotions are not rational. During those terrible days, there was nothing Dad could have done to save any one of them. Who lived or died depended on a roll of the dice.

After his return to Budapest, Dad kept writing tear-jerking letters telling me he was saving money to bring me back to him. Thank God his plans never came to fruition. My uncle and aunt read all correspondence between my father and me. In my eyes, they censored our letters. I thought, wait a minute, my father wrote these letters to me, not to this family, so why are you all reading it?

The letters I had written him were also censored. There was no private communication between us. While I resented it, I was unable to say so. I could not take the chance of offending my new family. If I disagreed, perhaps they would no longer want me.

Although, as prearranged, Dad got his business back, the Russians soon confiscated it when the country turned Communist and the Iron Curtain dropped. Nevertheless, he was happy about the Russian occupation. He had feared that without their presence the Nazis would regain power. Even today, strong anti-Semitism exists in Hungary.

We thought one of the reasons he wanted to return to Hungary was his lady friend, Hermina. In a short while, however, he married Gabriella, a woman with a son and a daughter. He not only had a new wife but also a new daughter. The daughter, Cica (Kitty), was my age. As I saw it, my father not only had deserted me, but also replaced me with another little girl. I corresponded with Dad sporadically, but the love and warmth I had once felt for him was gone forever. Since I've grown up, I've wondered many times whether I would have been happier being with him once he remarried and brought a stepmother and other children into the house. I really don't think so. My lot in life was cast by the loss of my mother.

When the war was over, my father was only in his late forties. He needed to remarry. Of course, as a child, I couldn't see that. Dad was only sixty-two years old when he passed away on January 28, 1960. He suffered through a long, drawn-out illness. At first it was thought he had had a stroke, but as his illness progressed and he lost his eyesight, the doctors realized that he actually had a malignant brain tumor. Interestingly, my cousin Paul, who was a medical student at the time, diagnosed my father's symptoms correctly long before the Hungarian attending physicians. Pneumonia set in and took him to his final resting place. To the best of my knowledge, Gabriella was a very caring wife and took good care of him throughout his long illness, but Gabriella and I never built a relationship that would continue after my father's demise.

CHAPTER V
GROWING UP IN AMERICA

Soon after our arrival in the United States, I was enrolled in Stone Elementary School and started in the third grade. I was a novelty. Little children are the best teachers as they speak a simple language. They gathered around me every chance they had, teaching me one word at a time. As my English improved, I was promoted to higher grades. My European education put me way ahead in math, science and languages, except English. I stayed at Stone School for one year, one semester longer than if I had been born here. By the time I graduated, I was able to get up on the podium and give a speech.

I was a chubby, overweight teenager, and my family felt it was imperative that I lose weight. My cousins teased me about my size. My uncle attributed my overeating to the lack of food during the war. That could not have been further from the truth. I never starved. The available food may not have been to my liking, but I never went hungry. The truth is that once my mother died, the only pleasure in my life was eating. This started in Hungary and continued in the United States. I missed my mother and father, and I ate to compensate for the emptiness in my heart.

While at Stone School, my cousin Tom and I went home for lunch. Paul was already in high school. Tom sat down with two big bologna sandwiches covered with lettuce, tomatoes and mayo, while I got dry cottage cheese and green peppers. I drooled as I watched Tom eat. Of course, this was all done for my benefit. As a child, I could not see it that way. It didn't feel good. My self-esteem hit rock bottom. I was a worthless fat girl. So, when I washed the dinner dishes, I grabbed some bread, wiped out the drippings from the roaster and gobbled it down before anyone could catch me. One evening, I found a bag of walnuts in the pantry. I was stuffing my mouth by the handful when my aunt came by and quietly said, "Good night, Agnes."

She never said another word about it. She didn't have to; she got her point across. I felt humiliated.

Senn High School followed. Adolescence was difficult enough without the insecurity and loneliness I felt. My feelings vacillated between gratitude and resentment toward my uncle and aunt. There is a very fine line separating these emotions. I desperately wanted to refer to them as Mom and Dad rather than Aunt and Uncle. I wanted to share their last name. I needed to feel like a normal kid with a mom and dad. However, no matter how I tried, I felt I was a disappointment to them. I was a good student and brought home good grades, but that didn't count; I was chubby and my worth depended on whether I weighed a couple of pounds more or less. The scale became my enemy. While in high school, my aunt packed lunches for Paul, Tom and me to take to school. Now my lunch consisted of a hard-boiled egg, a green pepper and an apple for dessert. Conforming is very important to teens. I wanted to be just like my friends. Why couldn't I have a sandwich like the others at my table were eating?

Sometimes I felt I was an embarrassment to my new family. I received mixed signals. Supposedly I was part of this family, but I never truly belonged. No matter what, I was always on the outside looking in. During these turbulent years, I discovered Dr. Norman Vincent Peale's book, *The Power of Positive Thinking*. I found solace in his writing. I missed the unconditional love all children are entitled to and deserve from their parents. Growing up is not easy for either the parent or the child. The teen years are a time of rebellion.

I never felt secure enough in my place in the Kuhn family to say no to anything asked of me. I constantly wondered what would happen if I said no. Would they throw me out in the street? Expressing my feelings was taboo. Sure, they told me they loved me, but did they really? Sibling rivalry for the love of a parent is common. I was not a sibling, so how did I fit into this picture? As a teenager, these thoughts haunted me.

Aunt Betsy and Uncle Eugene's friend, a Hungarian physician, Dr. Louis Singer, befriended me and took me under his wings during my teens. He invited me to his office just to talk. The words gushed forth. I am not sure why, but I trusted him. I had a desperate need to open up and allow my feelings to surface. Each time he listened to me intently. I always felt better after I left his office. He offered a release for my pent-up emotions. He never asked me to step on a scale, and that alone was a relief. I've wondered many times whether our conversations remained private or did he report back to my uncle and aunt. It no longer matters.

In nice weather, my friends and I frequently walked home from high school. We often stopped for snacks along the way. On a sunshiny spring day, I bought a double dip ice cream cone. My friend Sylvia came into my house with me. Somehow, the conversation led to food. Sylvia opened her big mouth and said, "You had a double dip ice cream cone on the way home." I am sure she didn't realize the anguish and embarrassment her words caused me. I wished the floor had opened and swallowed me.

During my early high school days, I had a steady babysitting job Saturday nights and made $2.00 an evening. It was sufficient spending money for me. In 1949, after I turned sixteen, I got a part time job at a neighborhood dime store and later cashiered at a Spiegel retail store downtown at State and Madison. I worked after school Mondays and Thursdays until 9:00 P.M. and all day Saturdays. When the store closed at 9:00 P.M., I got on the subway and headed home. At the Granville station, I transferred to a bus that took me to the corner of Devon and Claremont. We lived a half a block from there, and I walked home. Nobody worried about a young girl riding the L and the bus at night. Those were different, safer times.

My friends and I ice skated at Touhy Beach during the winter and rode our bikes when weather permitted. We also enjoyed listening to music at a record shop at Devon and Western where we could take a record into a booth, listen to it and then return it to the attendant.

In the spring, huge trucks unloaded the annual carnival in an empty lot near my house. With great anticipation, we watched them drop off and set up various booths and rides. There was no Disneyland. As teenagers, this was our opportunity to have fun.

Until I came to the United States, I had virtually no contact with boys. I had no brothers and I went to all-girl schools. I found it very difficult to interact with the opposite sex. My girl friends became boy crazy. While I too longed for a boyfriend, I did not know how to flirt. It did not come naturally to me as it did to most American girls who grew up in a culture where they intermingled with boys from an early age. Paul brought home his friends, a bunch of cute guys, but they didn't even notice me, let alone talk to me. As I got further into my teens, I became more withdrawn and self-conscious. My friends were dating, and I had no boy friends. No boy friends, no dates equaled depression. More and more I turned to food as my sole source of pleasure. I shied away from social situations. My mother had died and deserted me, my father had gone back to Europe and deserted me; I must have done something terrible for everyone I loved to have deserted me. Consequently, I was worthless.

I spent four wonderful summers at Camp Lake of the Woods in Decatur, Michigan. Those were the best times of my teens or perhaps even the best times of my life. Camp was a place where I felt accepted, where nobody sat in judgment, a place where everyone cheered and nobody jeered, a place of lasting friendships and wonderful memories. But, while camp was the greatest, the feeling of being the odd one out still lingered. I was grateful that I was able to be there, but it was embarrassing and demeaning that I had to set tables before meals in order to help pay my tuition. At that age, I didn't have the wisdom to consider the financial burden I was on the Kuhn family. After all, my father had told me that everyone was rich in America. I wondered if I were part of this family, why I was the only one who had to supplement my tuition, even in a small way, while my cousins' tuitions were paid. The question of whether I really belonged followed me even to camp.

My high school friends were preparing to go to college, but no one ever discussed that possibility with me. My cousins were going to college, and I wanted to go too. Actually, I wanted to become a doctor like Aunt Etta, but I was unable to convey my desire to anyone. I now realize that financially medical school would not have been feasible. I even consulted with my high school's guidance counselor and asked for her help in figuring out how I could attend college. I told her that Paul was going to the University of Chicago before graduating high school. Her only advice was, "Finish high school and worry about college later." At that time, I knew nothing of scholarships or working one's way through school.

Uncle Eugene insisted I take some commercial courses such as typing, shorthand, and bookkeeping. He wanted me to become a secretary and work in an office upon graduation. This definitely was not what I wanted to do with my life. I had trouble learning to type and was told that I lacked coordination because I'd had polio as a young child. This was the first time I ever heard that I had polio. In Hungary, my friend's sister was in a wheelchair as a result of polio. I recall my legs being paralyzed or numb while I was very sick, but I was always under the impression that I had had scarlet fever.

While pondering my future, it struck me that if I could not become a doctor, perhaps I could be a nurse. That way, I could get an education while living away from home. I applied at Mt. Sinai Hospital's Nursing School. I was not only accepted but was offered a scholarship.

My two older cousins Peter and Paul went to the University of Chicago and became physicians. My younger cousin Tom went to Northwestern. After receiving his Bachelor's degree, contrary to his father's wishes, Tom headed for Hollywood and became Mr. Show Biz. He made a name for himself in the film industry and made his dream come true. All three of my cousins settled in California.

CHAPTER VI
HERE COMES THE BRIDE

During my senior year in high school, a schoolmate invited me to go on a double date with her and her boyfriend. That's how I met Danny Kittay, the son of a cantor. That evening once again changed the direction of my life. We immediately took a liking to each other. He was a good-looking young man with a thick head of blond, wavy hair. I liked his sense of humor. When he spoke, there was something in his voice that said, "I really like you." His touch electrified me.

He lived in Hyde Park on the South Side of Chicago, while I lived up north. Side. In spite of the many miles between us, within a short time he became a nightly visitor. It was an exciting time for me. After all, there was a boy in the world who liked me just the way I was and didn't care I wasn't a size seven. He was an "older guy," already out in the working world, not just another high school boy. He always had something nice and flattering to say and seldom came to the door without some trinket, candy or flowers. When we met, Danny was almost twenty-two and I was almost eighteen. He was an electronic technician, a recent graduate of DeVry Technical Institute. Television was in its infancy and good technicians were in great demand. Our romance blossomed and within six weeks he asked me to marry him. It was a fairy tale come true. I went to school and told my friend that Danny asked me to marry him. She became all excited and asked, "And what did you say?"

"I said I would."

Before I had a chance to give it a second thought, the news spread like wildfire, "Agnes is engaged." I became an overnight celebrity. It all happened so fast. I got caught up in a whirlwind of attention. My friends were only going to college, but I was getting married!

I got an engagement ring for my eighteenth birthday in July 1951, and the following month I graduated from high school. The diamond in my ring was hardly bigger than the head of a pin, but that didn't matter. Danny and the ring were both mine, all mine. My nursing career was totally forgotten. I was in love like no one had ever loved before.

Danny had come to rescue me from an unhappy home where I felt unloved and unwanted. He was going to make a home for us. It was the part of the fairy tale where the prince on the white horse rescues the maiden in distress. I never doubted his love for me and I was sure that one day he would give me everything I ever wanted. I had absolutely no perception of the correlation between higher education and a better living. Nobody had made any attempt to explain that to me. However, I must admit that no matter what anyone might have said, I probably would not have listened. While my family was not thrilled with my upcoming marriage, especially at such a young age, I also sensed they were glad to be rid of me.

My aunt invited Danny's family for a get-acquainted dinner where my future father-in-law said, "Agnes is such a lucky girl to marry a nice American boy."

This did not sit well with Aunt Betsy. She answered him, "At age eighteen she is not exactly an old maid."

While both families were cordial, it was obvious they had very little in common and the two would never meld.

On October 28, 1951, I proudly became Mrs. Daniel Kittay. Aunt Betsy and Uncle Eugene threw a small, elegant wedding for us at the Shoreland Hotel. Only the immediate family was invited. I wore a blue dress; cinnamon colored shoes, purse and hat with a veil Aunt Betsy bought for me. Of course, the blue dress was more practical than a wedding gown; it could be worn on other occasions. Secretly, I wished for a wedding gown. Tom sang while Aunt Betsy played the wedding march on the piano as I walked down the aisle on Uncle Eugene's arm. While my uncle and aunt shared this special day with me, they made it very clear that once I said, "I do" I passed the point of no return and I was on my own.

CHAPTER VII
THE JOYS OF MARRIAGE

Our first love nest was at 5120 South Harper. It was a one-room with kitchenette apartment. The Murphy bed, when not in use, folded into the wall. I found a job at a neighborhood bank. Life was filled with many new experiences. At the supermarket, I bought a bright red delicious-looking steak. With loving care I seasoned it, broiled it, and served it on a new white platter. To my great disappointment, it was impossible to chew. I had my first cooking lesson: round steak may look delicious, but it's not for broiling.

Our kind but very nosy neighbor Mrs. Levy raised parakeets. She truly tried to be helpful. When I had the stomach flu, we knew she was standing in front of the door listening to our conversation. Danny said jokingly, "Honey, maybe you're pregnant. We could soon become parents."

Mrs. Levy wasted no time. She knocked on the door with her revelation, "You know, Agnes, you might be feeling sick to your stomach because you're pregnant."

We had a good laugh after she left.

On a Friday evening, we had invited some friends for dinner. I made a fancy dessert in my new jello mold. The mold had grooves on the outside for warm water to help separate the jello from the mold. As directed, I placed a plate over the mold, turned it upside down and poured warm water in the grooves. The jello, however, stuck stubbornly and wouldn't come out. Frustrated, I picked up the mold, without the plate under it, and carried it to the sink. Big mistake. The jello dropped all over the floor. I wiped up the jello, put it in a brown bag, and asked Danny to throw it down the garbage chute while I cleaned up the floor. Danny and his buddy came back from the garbage chute laughing, telling us the bag broke and the jello went all over the floor. I was sure they were joking and laughed along with them. Next morning, my face turned red as I heard the janitor swear at whoever dropped the jello on the floor and didn't clean it up.

I was the world's worst housekeeper. Since there was nobody to tell me what to do, I did as I pleased. Of course, I soon learned that my newly found independence came with many new responsibilities, such as paying bills. Danny and I ate as we pleased and we both got fatter and fatter. He loved me anyway. At last, I was number one again in someone's life. I didn't realize until many years later the importance of being top priority to someone. It was a good feeling, a feeling I had longed for since the war. I couldn't imagine life without my husband.

I knew before we married that Danny did not come from a happy home. My mother-in-law and father-in-law lived a very different lifestyle from the one I had experienced. They lived under the same roof, but certainly not together. Actually, their marriage was very unhappy. They were both extremely controlling individuals. At first, I enjoyed the attention they showered on me. As time went on, however, our lives became a fish bowl. What first appeared to be love and concern turned to intrusion into our daily lives.

Danny had an older brother and a younger sister. They lived in opposite corners of the United States, Joe in Seattle, Washington and Frances in Long Island, New York. We were the only children in Chicago and Mom and Dad Kittay had far too much time to spend on us. Danny disliked the Chicago winters and resented his parents' meddling. He thought we could escape both by moving south. Houston was a burgeoning town with many opportunities. We decided to investigate a possible move. Danny went to Texas for a first-hand look at the job market as well as living conditions. He returned full of enthusiasm.

In January 1952, we packed our belongings and moved to Houston. Life was truly an adventure, a constant honeymoon. Upon our arrival, we lived at various motels. For $5 a night, we could get a clean, standard motel room. Once, we tried to save money by renting a $3 room. As soon as we opened the door and saw bugs crawling, we turned around and walked out. It was well worth the extra $2 to stay in a clean place. Eventually, the nightly motel stays became expensive, and it was time to find a permanent residence. We moved into the second floor apartment of a recently built two-bedroom duplex. Homes and apartments were cooled by attic fans or ceiling fans. Only the very rich had air conditioning. After we got settled, we set out to find a good location to open our television repair shop. We found our spot on Telephone Road.

We adopted a deserted, homeless calico kitten and named her Genevieve. The three of us, Danny, Genevieve, and I rode together daily to and from the store.

We made friends with a gentleman who ran the projector at the neighborhood movie. He gave us passes to all the shows. The air conditioning in the movie was a delightful respite in the hot and humid climate.

Living in the South was an education. I found the separate water fountains and washrooms for whites and blacks appalling. Our only employee was a black man, a talented technician, who worked for a pittance because that's the way "colored folks" were paid in the Houston area. Besides, that was all we could afford. He was a clean, friendly, well-mannered gentleman with excellent skills. Our neighbors at the store were in the jewelry business and had moved to Houston from Southern Illinois. Our stores shared a washroom. To my amazement, the jeweler and his wife complained to the landlord about a black man using the facilities. This was a world I had never known. What happened to the land of the free?

On weekends, Danny and I walked through the parks, watched the children play and admired every baby. We were so very young and naive! We rationalized that if we liked babies, why not have one of our own? It was not long after we made this decision that I started throwing up very regularly, not only in the morning, but around the clock. We should have bought stock in the makers of Alka Seltzer. I had constant heartburn, and plop, plop, fizz, fizz, I lived on Alka Seltzers. The medical profession had not yet determined that taking medication while carrying a child was unsafe. While pregnancy was no piece of cake, nine months later, in January 1953 my first child, Steven Michael, was born. One look at him made any discomfort endured during pregnancy and delivery worthwhile. He was the most beautiful baby on earth. It never occurred to either Danny or me that our baby might be born with a birth defect. We counted his fingers and toes and took it for granted that we had a healthy, perfect baby. I will never forget the look of awe on my husband's face when he looked at our child.

I loved my family. I loved life.

I had worked at our TV repair store until Steve was born. We were finally beginning to show a profit. After the baby arrived, I stayed home. My help at the store was greatly missed. There was no one to answer the telephone or keep the store open while Danny made service calls. We could not afford another salary. After struggling for a few months to keep the business going, we gave up, locked the door for the last time and returned the key to the landlord.

When Steve was seven months old, we packed up our station wagon and returned to Chicago. The crib mattress fit perfectly across the back seat. There were no car seats or seat belts to fasten. Steve gurgled happily as he rolled around while we traveled. We arrived in Chicago broke, moved in with Grandma and Grandpa Kittay for a few months until we saved enough to pay a security deposit and a month's rent.

It was a great day when we were able to move into a place of our own. Our apartment, located above a store, had three bedrooms, a living room, a dining room, a large kitchen and one bathroom with old-fashioned fixtures. The bathtub stood on legs and it was hard to clean under it. One of the bedrooms had no windows while the windows of the rear bedroom opened onto an enclosed porch. The living room and the front bedroom faced the street. It wasn't a palace, but it was a home of our own.

My second child, William Allen, was born in August 1956 and my daughter, Cheryl Margaret, came into the world in September 1957. They were both born at Chicago's Woodlawn Hospital.

CHAPTER VIII
DANNY'S ACCIDENT

Although during the week Danny was employed as a technician at a TV repair shop, he earned extra money evenings and weekends by servicing his private customers.

The day we intended to tell the family we were expecting our third baby, Danny had dropped our two children and me off at the home of Aunt Johanna, Grandma Kittay's sister. He had scheduled a service call and planned to join us when he was done. We waited for hours for his arrival and knew something had to be wrong when he didn't get there. Finally, Grandma, Grandpa and I took the children home. The phone was ringing as we walked in the door. It was an ambulance chaser informing me that Danny had been hit by a car and seriously injured. My husband had already been operated on for multiple fractures of his leg. He also suffered a concussion and multiple lacerations. The caller offered to pick me up and take me to the hospital. Grandpa felt it wouldn't be prudent to get in a car with a stranger. I was so shaken I couldn't think. Terrible thoughts flashed through my mind. Will he survive? Will he be able to walk again? Will he be able to work again? What will I do with two children and one on the way if he should die or become unable to take care of us? Life without him was unimaginable.

We called a cab, and Grandpa and I headed for South Chicago Hospital. Grandma stayed behind with the children.

Now, as a mother of grown children, I realize how difficult it must have been for her to stay with the children so I could go to my husband. My darling was badly hurt. He was hospitalized about six weeks and was discharged on crutches with a cast up to his hip. These were rough financial times. He was out of work most of the year. I had two small children, a third one on the way, a husband on crutches and no income.

Grandma's salary as a secretary at Michael Reese Hospital was not designed to support a family of four plus herself. In spite of her meager earnings, she helped us pay our rent and put food on the table. Uncle Eugene loaned us $200. Through his recommendation, we retained a prominent attorney to proceed against the driver of the automobile.

In 1958, our pending lawsuit against the culpable driver was finally settled. When disbursements were made, I questioned a $200 deduction from the proceeds. The attorney advised us that Uncle Eugene had put a lien on the monies he lent us, to be deducted and repaid at the resolution of the lawsuit. It was humiliating that he didn't trust us for $200. Grandma Kittay said we owed her nothing. We used the money from the settlement for a down payment on a home.

Our neighbor Jim worked for a trucking company. Once Danny was able to drive, Jim got him a job as a dispatcher. He was able to sit while working and did not have to move around. By the time Cheryl arrived, a leg brace replaced Danny's cast and he was able to drive and navigate with more ease. Considering the seriousness of his injuries, he had made an excellent recovery.

CHAPTER IX
A HOME OF OUR OWN

We searched for a home of our own and found an appealing three-bedroom model home, within our price range, on the corner of 92nd Street and Chappel, across the street from Warren Elementary School. There were three empty lots adjacent to the model. We contracted for a home to be built and by summer, our three-bedroom ranch-style dream house was ready for occupancy. We enrolled Steve in kindergarten at Warren Elementary School. I was able to stand on the porch or at the window and watch him cross the street to school. The principal told me, "You are brave to buy a home across the street from a school. The kids will trample your grass."

I laughed, "I bought the home deliberately at this location so I could watch my child safely cross the street."

Those were some of the best days of my adult life. I had a loving husband, three children I adored and a home of our own. We didn't have much money, but that really didn't matter. I was sure that eventually Danny would make a good living for us.

Our neighbors were young adults with small children. It was a friendly community. Soon we felt quite comfortable in our new surroundings. The area offered suburban-style living with city conveniences. Most of the women were stay-at-home moms, good friends who looked out for each other's children. Our neighbors became our extended families.

CHAPTER X
STORMY WEATHER

In 1964, during the thirteenth year of our marriage, I felt something was wrong. Incidents that bordered on the bizarre had occurred. Danny worked for a trade school, selling as well as teaching electronics courses. He worked long hours and usually didn't get home much before midnight. Jack Paar, the host of the Tonight Show, kept me company while I waited for Danny. I came alive when I heard his key in the door. I warmed up and served him dinner as we chatted about the happenings of the day. He started telling me strange stories, that Jerry, the owner of the business, had the school's telephones bugged. Danny cautioned me against discussing anything personal over the phone. As time went by, he became more and more agitated, believing spies were following him. For years, Danny had found occult books fascinating. He started to read the Kabala and lost himself in this book of Jewish mysticism. He believed that other people knew what he was thinking. He accused me of reading his mind and sharing this information with others. I was too naive to realize that his strange behavior was a symptom of a terrible mental illness. One Sunday I talked him into visiting his cousin Bernice and her physician husband, Oscar. By this time, I was sure that something was very wrong, and I needed a professional opinion to validate my thinking. Oscar quickly confirmed my suspicions and told me to get Danny to a psychiatrist as quickly as possible. I soon discovered that it is not easy to get an adult to a doctor when the patient firmly believes there is absolutely nothing wrong with him.

During the dreadful upheaval that followed, Bernice and Oscar became my dearest friends and allies. They were the only ones I could talk to about the constantly changing, unstable situation in my home. They truly understood and never doubted my word. I could not have made it without their moral support. Sometimes Bernice and I talked six or seven times a day. She never said, "I am too busy to talk right now," in spite of the fact that she, too, had small children. I always have been grateful for Bernice and Oscar's support. Through the years, we have maintained a close relationship. We may not talk as often as we used to, but the warmth and empathy remains between us. We are still "cousins." Oscar is still my medical consultant.

Danny's sister Fran and her husband Gene came for a visit from New York. After spending an evening with Danny and me, they felt that I was the one who acted troubled and sat with a long face while Danny told jovial anecdotes. Of course I was upset and depressed; I knew his stories did not deal with reality. They did not understand that his "funny stories" were a manifestation of his illness.

The day Danny called and threatened to jump off the top of the Prudential Building, I became desperate. There was no time to plan or ponder; I had to get him help immediately. That evening, with the help of Uncle Leo and Aunt Johanna, Grandma Kittay's sister and her husband, I managed to take Danny to the emergency room of Michael Reese, a hospital with an excellent psychiatric unit. Aunt Johanna stayed with my bewildered children while Uncle Leo drove us. I had not learned to drive. Grandma worked at that hospital and had some connections; however, she really did not understand the nature or severity of Danny's illness. Her main concern was, "What will the neighbors think?"

It took the psychiatrist only a few minutes to evaluate the situation. Danny needed immediate hospitalization. The doctor gave him the option of being voluntarily admitted to Michael Reese Hospital or being committed to a state mental institution. Danny reluctantly agreed to be admitted to Michael Reese Hospital's Psychiatric Unit. He was told he had had a nervous breakdown, and he took that expression literally. He believed that his nerves were physically broken. This theory fit his paranoiac belief that strangers were chasing him and harming him. He spent several weeks as an inpatient receiving medication and therapy. Anti-psychotic drugs were in their early stages. A highly skilled empathetic young psychiatrist, Dr. Ned Cowan, was charged with treating him and following his progress.

Dr. Cowan suggested I seek supportive therapy from the Jewish Family Service. I was fortunate to be assigned to a motherly, very capable, caring social worker. She slowly, and often very painfully, led me to understand my situation and helped me explore my options.

Therapy became a useful tool, enabling me to understand and unravel the events in my life that had brought me to this point.

When I asked Dr. Cowan for a diagnosis, he said, "We treat symptoms and don't like to put labels on patients." I had a layman's paperback medical book at home. I made my own diagnosis as the symptoms in the book fit Danny perfectly. Dear God, he is a paranoid schizophrenic, I thought to myself. When I confronted Dr. Cowan with my diagnosis, he could not deny it. He explained that it is possible for a patient to have a single acute episode and then become himself again. I started reading anything and everything I could find about this illness. None of it was encouraging. A British doctor wrote that sometimes schizophrenia occurs between two people. He was so right! I was the catalyst and the illness manifested itself between Danny and me. At that time, he was still able to behave quite normally in the presence of others. I also read that most mass murderers are paranoid schizophrenics and I began to worry about my family's safety.

I realized that much of Danny's behavior, which I believed to have been mere idiosyncrasies, dated back to the time we were newlyweds. Perhaps if I had been a bit older and wiser when we married, I would have picked up on signs of mental illness earlier.

Soon after we married, I had had a telephone conversation with my aunt. While we chatted, I told her that Danny and I went to the neighborhood movie. After I hung up the phone, Danny asked, "Why did you have to tell her where we went?" I didn't give it a second thought at the time, but now I know that he was already showing signs of paranoia. His "idiosyncrasies" were actually a precursor of his total breakdown.

Dr. Cowan said, "The best we can hope for is recovery to his condition prior to his total loss of contact with reality." I certainly would have happily settled for that.

About six weeks after his admission, our visits became easier and more pleasant as our conversations became more realistic. We were now discussing Danny's homecoming, returning to work, and taking care of his family. Before his discharge, the doctor explained that with the proper medication, Danny might be able to function and might never have another acute episode.

I asked the doctor, "Wouldn't Danny recognize the symptoms if he should regress?"

Dr. Cowan replied, "Not necessarily."

He was so right. With high hopes and a big smile, I took Danny home to our children who stood at the window waiting for him with great anticipation. For a brief time, Danny returned to work, and our lives resumed some degree of normalcy.

CHAPTER XI
LIFE WITH A PARANOID SCHIZOPHRENIC

Unfortunately, one of the symptoms of this horrible illness, schizophrenia, is that the patient believes he is in step, while the rest of the world is out of step. Insisting there was nothing wrong with him, Danny soon decided that he didn't need to take his medication. Without it, his condition quickly worsened. He quit one job after another because he believed people could read his mind. Even worse, he blamed me for knowing what he was thinking and sharing his thoughts with the rest of the world. Once again, I was the focal point of his paranoia. I asked the doctor, "Could I crush his medication and hide it in his coffee?"

Dr. Cowan answered, "You must not do that because if he finds out, in his state of paranoia, he will think you are trying to poison him."

Danny could sit in a room filled with people and stare into space, totally detached. Steve was about thirteen at that time. He was the only one of my three children old enough to understand what was happening. At times, Steve's eyes would meet mine as if to acknowledge that we both knew Daddy was in another world.

It became clear that the financial support of my family would fall on me, probably sooner rather than later. The Jewish Vocational Service came to my assistance. After some vocational testing, they undertook the expense of sending me to Beverly Business College. Not only did they pay for my tuition and books, but even paid my carfare. My will provides a small endowment to the Jewish Vocational Service, earmarked for the education of a needy person.

It was either school or welfare. Fate played a cruel joke on me. The Jewish Federation wanted to send me to a university to become a teacher or a social worker. Now somebody wanted to send me to college, and I no longer had the opportunity to take advantage of it. There was no time; I knew I didn't have the luxury of attending school for four years before I had to earn a living.

CHAPTER XII
MOM GOES BACK TO SCHOOL

Going to school served a dual purpose. Not only did I learn new skills, but also my mind was kept so busy. I had less time to brood and worry. The first morning I cried all the way to school after leaving my three children home to get themselves off to school without my help. Every noon I called to see how they were doing. My calls were always answered with various complaints, such as, "My brother pulled my hair," or "Tell her to stop teasing me." I tried to make peace. I was aware that their complaints were exaggerated, and there was nothing I could do about their squabbling. They were letting me know they wanted me at home. I repeatedly told myself, wipe away your tears, Agnes, and go back to the books. Your decision was based on necessity, not choice.

The Kittay family blamed me for anything and everything. I had no one to turn to for comfort. I was so distraught that I seriously considered suicide. There was no point to living if I couldn't take care of my children. Turning on the gas jets and going to sleep forever seemed to be the easiest solution. I asked myself, what would my children do without me? I knew I couldn't abandon them, and I surely couldn't take them along.

The only person who offered me any help was Josephine, my old babysitter. She said, "Mrs. Kittay, I don't have much, but if you ever need money to feed these children, I will help you." I have never forgotten her kindness and I am glad I never had to accept her offer.

Uncle Eugene did offer to assist in finding the proper charity to help us. His words stung so badly that they are etched into my mind with acid. Then, to add insult to injury, he mumbled something about, "Well, of course, if you were our child. . ." Perhaps his words enabled me and gave me the courage to help myself. Right then and there, I decided I would rather starve than ask him for anything. I never did.

During this turmoil, I learned to drive with the help of neighbors and friends. Oscar's pediatric practice was growing, and he and Bernice offered me their old Volkswagen for the cost of a repair, which I paid off in installments. I knew nothing about maintaining an automobile. A little green light on the dashboard kept blinking at me. Since the light was green, I presumed it was a good sign and didn't worry about it. One evening, as I exited the Calumet Expressway with my children, I heard a terrible banging noise and pulled into the nearest gas station. The attendant scratched his head as he said: "Lady, don't you ever check the oil in this car? The engine is bone dry. You threw a rod." I had no idea what he meant. I never thought of checking the oil. Because of my stupidity, I destroyed the engine and ruined my car. What a blow. I needed to find other affordable means of transportation.

My self-confidence grew in proportion with the knowledge I gained. I had the best neighbors and friends anyone could ever have. They were all stay-at-home mothers. I knew I could always count on my neighbors, Carol and Artie. When I could not be home, I knew my children could turn to them in case of emergency. Carol and Artie, I am eternally grateful for your friendship and help.

Danny bounced in and out of Michael Reese Hospital's psychiatric unit. The pattern continued. When on medication, he functioned; once home, he refused medication and went downhill again. His condition was no longer a single acute episode. He had become chronically ill. Michael Reese Hospital's program was designed for patients with acute, not chronic, mental problems. Danny no longer qualified for treatment.

In the meantime, the army called up Dr. Cowan and another young psychiatrist was assigned to care for Danny. This doctor made it clear that he couldn't risk his patient-physician confidentiality with Danny and refused to talk to me. Of course, his decision made my life even more difficult.

Since Danny refused medical care, I repeatedly went to court to have him committed to a state mental hospital. Commitment procedures are difficult. I had to prove that he was either a danger to himself or to others. The social worker from the Jewish Family Service went to court with me for moral support. The judge ordered Danny committed to Kankakee State Hospital where he received medication but little or no therapy. I have read that medication is the established standard of care and that therapy in chronic cases of schizophrenia is really useless. As soon as Danny was discharged, this cycle repeated.

It is impossible to describe what it is like to be married to someone with this horrendous illness. Life becomes totally unpredictable. There is no sleeping; there is no certainty about anything.

In October 1965, during one of Danny's several hospitalizations at Kankakee, his father passed away. Grandpa had a pacemaker surgically inserted in his chest to regulate his heartbeat. He had an uneventful recovery until the day of his expected discharge. Then, he was diagnosed with hepatitis from tainted blood received in a transfusion. The hepatitis in his weakened post-operative condition killed him. After he died, he instantly became a saint to his bereaved widow, my mother-in-law. One would have thought from the way she carried on that theirs was the greatest marriage. I have seen this phenomenon repeatedly in my life, that when a spouse from a bad marriage dies, he or she suddenly becomes an angel to the widow or widower. We humans have a tendency to forget the bad times and remember the good.

I went to Kankakee to bring Danny home for his father's funeral. The death of his father didn't seem to faze him. At the funeral, he appeared stoic and showed no emotion. However, on the way home from the cemetery, we found Inky, our black cat, dead in the street. Danny became hysterical over the loss of our pet. Perhaps it took the sight of the mangled cat to unleash his emotions.

There was no stability in our home. The children felt it and their behavior reflected their insecurity. I watched my husband who, not long before had been my best friend, my confidant and my lover turn into a totally erratic stranger whose behavior became more and more irrational and unpredictable. After many counseling sessions, I finally was able to make the decision to get a divorce. Since I was unable to help Danny, I needed to direct my efforts towards creating a stable environment for my children. The guilt of leaving my husband solely because he was sick was overwhelming. He was neither a drunkard nor a womanizer and did not possess any of the terrible qualities that often cause women to seek divorces. He was just sick, so terribly sick. The look on the faces of mental health professionals told the story. When I said, "paranoid schizophrenic," their chins dropped. Would I think of leaving him if he had cancer, heart disease, or any other physical ailment? Of course not. However, this was different, very, very different. I had not only lost my husband, the father of my children and our breadwinner, but I had also lost my family, my in-laws.

I still remember the look in my Steve's eyes when his birthday neared and he awaited an annual gift from his Auntie Frances, Danny's sister. He was certain she would not forget his birthday. No she did not forget; the gift simply never came. Grandma Kittay explained that it would be too difficult for me to reciprocate. How do you explain this to a thirteen year old?

Our hearts break when our children hurt.

Before the finale of the marriage, I was actually raped by my husband. What a horrible end to something that started out as such a great love. Danny had totally lost control of himself in every respect. That evening, he picked up the Yellow Pages and tore the book in half. He was not a large man, but his sickness gave him frightening power. We had sex before going to sleep. He awakened me in the middle of the night, forcing himself upon me and into me. He had never been aggressive before. I knew this was his illness taking over. Nevertheless, it was a horrible experience. A couple hours later, he spontaneously ejaculated again.

The following day, we went to see Dr. Cowan. First Danny saw him alone, and then we talked to the doctor together. Before I had a chance to say anything, the doctor told me about the positive visit he had with my husband. It is amazing how a schizophrenic can mask his behavior even to his psychiatrist. Of course, when I told the doctor what happened the previous night, he no longer thought Danny was doing so well. Once again, he was committed to a state hospital.

Through all this, I learned that as far as the law is concerned only the patients' rights are considered and protected. No one cares about the family's plight. But, heaven forbid that patient should be hospitalized or ordered to take medication against his will. That's a violation of his civil rights. When we protect every mentally ill person's right not to be hospitalized or be given medication against his will, we also protect the right to refuse help to people incapable of making a rational decision. I don't think our founding fathers had this in mind when they wrote the Constitution. It seems to me that the patient's civil rights would be much better served by enforcing some type of medication program so that the patient could stay with his family and remain a productive member of society. As an alternative, the patient becomes a street person, likely to be dangerous to himself as well as to others. When that happens, we have indeed robbed these people of their civil rights that would enable them to lead useful lives.

Danny's first discharge from Michael Reese Hospital was called a "conditional discharge." It obligated him to remain on his prescribed medication and visit his psychiatrist regularly. Conditional discharges no longer exist because the courts ruled they violate the patient's civil rights. I am a great advocate of civil rights, but this is sheer insanity! In the meantime, the courts have totally forgotten that families of mental patients also have civil rights, i.e., living in peace without fear. No law enforcement agency is empowered to look out for the safety of the families. Something terrible, such as murder, must take place before the police can step in.

CHAPTER XIII
WORKING MOTHER

In 1966, while still married, I graduated from Beverly Business College at the top of my class. When it became a necessity, I had no problem learning to type, first on a manual typewriter and later on an electric machine. There were no computers. For multiple copies, we used carbon paper. If there was a typo, several copies had to be erased. I became an excellent stenographer, typist and bookkeeper. It was time to find a job and test my skills in the real world.

Wilson & Company, the meat packers, with offices in the Prudential Building, offered me a job as secretary to Bill Gray, Manager of the Beef Department. I sincerely believe that I was the only Jewish employee on their large payroll. However, when I asked for time off to observe the Jewish Holidays, my boss made sure that the holidays were not charged against my vacation days. During the three years I worked for him, Bill Gray never said "good morning," "good night," or "go to hell." He spoke only the absolute necessities. I never got to know him as a person; there was no small talk between us. I started with a salary of $100 per week. After taxes, I took home $88.88. For a brief time, there were two paychecks. We were able to save my salary while we lived on Danny's earnings.

During our marriage, even before his illness surfaced, Danny quit one job after another. He always wanted to go into sales, but never succeeded in that field. He was often out of work because of his desire to pursue various other careers. During these periods, Grandma always came to our rescue and paid our bills. She bought the majority of our children's clothes, including winter coats. While I was young, I took her help for granted, never realizing that she should have been saving money for her old age. Taking from her had become a way of life. Since she was the only model of a mother in my life, I thought that's what all parents did for their children. Once our marriage was in trouble, she cut off her help. I think she had hoped that my financial dependence would keep me from going through with the divorce. I not only lost my husband, but for the third time in my life, I also lost my family.

My children, thinking that after finishing school Mom would once again stay home, were very upset when I went to work. My daughter seemed to be affected most. Her grades plummeted. Luckily, she had a dedicated teacher who worked with me on getting her back on track. The bottom line was that my family was falling apart and my children were suffering, disturbed to the point where each had serious emotional problems. Reluctantly, I called the Chicago Bar Association and asked for a referral to a divorce attorney.

In July 1967, after fifteen years of marriage, the pounding of a judge's gavel ended my marriage and my hopes and dreams of a lifetime. I had $2,000 in the bank and a home in a neighborhood that was rapidly deteriorating. My neighbors all vowed they would not sell as one house after another went on the market. My monthly mortgage payments were $95. I really didn't want to move. I knew living elsewhere would be much more expensive. I tried to stall and kept delaying putting my home up for sale.

I learned that when a judge grants a divorce, it does not mean one is divorced emotionally. The latter is much more difficult. Danny often popped in unannounced and the children were always happy to see him. In a way, so was I. I also knew that none of us could begin to recover while we simulated family life. My neighbors joked about Danny doing various chores around the house that he was unwilling to do while we were married. Once when I got home, I found him in the shower. The children had let him in. I pondered, how do I tell my children that they cannot let their father into the house? How can I get them to understand? How can I, alone, cope with all these problems? Why was I spared while others perished during the Holocaust if I couldn't do better by my children? I had no mother, and now my children have no father. For a while, I received child support. With my salary and the child support, we got along. But, how long would Danny be able to work? I knew I couldn't count on his income. I needed to find a better paying job with more opportunity. With three years of office experience under my belt, I was ready to step up the career ladder.

CHAPTER XIV
BRODY & GORE

A little research revealed that law offices had the highest pay scales for secretaries. Consequently, I needed to find work at a law office, although during vocational counseling I had been specifically told I would not be happy or suited for work in such an environment. I had acquired excellent skills, but the Jewish Vocational Service erred on this assessment.

In pursuit of a better job, I went to an employment agency. They sent me to interview with the law firm of Brody & Gore. George Gore greeted me with a handshake and a broad smile. There were no forms to fill out or tests to take. He simply said, "Tell me about yourself."

I told him that I was a business college graduate with good typing and stenographic skills. I had been in the work force for three years. I was divorced with three children, and I needed a better paying job with a future. He offered me a job on the spot, and I accepted it. This job paid $10 a week more than I was making at the meat packing company.

The work was demanding, but very interesting. There was so much to learn, and my brain absorbed it like a sponge. I actually loved the atmosphere of the law office. Bob Brody, who dictated non-stop without taking a breath, needed someone to work half days on Saturdays, and I jumped at the opportunity to earn extra money. I packed up crayons, coloring books and homework to keep Cheryl busy and took her along to the office every Saturday. As I anticipated, soon the child support payments stopped and I was on my own. The Saturday work made the difference between survival and the poor house. After three months of employment, George Gore offered me a $25 per month raise. I remembered a line from my previous boss when he said, "Either a man deserves a decent raise or he doesn't deserve one at all."

Suddenly, I heard myself repeat this statement to George Gore. I had obviously taken him by surprise. He suggested I wait another month and then see him again. That's exactly what I did. I got the raise I deserved.

I have heard it said that when God closes one door, He opens another and I believe that's so. Bea, the woman who worked for many years as

Bob Brody's secretary and office manager retired, and I was chosen to replace her. My salary increased with the additional responsibilities. I felt needed in this office. I truly contributed and earned my keep. George Gore introduced me to a friend one day by simply stating, "This is Agnes. She runs the office." He made me feel ten feet tall. As my self-confidence grew, my weight dropped proportionately. I began to feel I was worth something after all.

George Gore, the handsome younger partner of the firm, became very ill. After being in remission for many years, his cancer returned and snuffed out his life when he was only in his late fifties. Before he died, my friend Lois and I went to visit him at the hospital. We walked out in tears. We were shocked to see how this tall, attractive man had deteriorated in a relatively short time. He died soon after our visit. I not only lost an employer, but a dear friend.

Bob Brody, the senior partner, was like a delicious hard roll, crusty on the outside but soft and mushy on the inside. Screaming at young attorneys was his technique of teaching them. I did my job, and he was good to me. Besides, I was the only one able to keep up with his dictation. The support staff had a fifteen-minute coffee break in the morning and another in the afternoon. One time, we stayed on a break a bit longer and he called me on it. I calmly said, "Look Mr. Brody, I don't watch the clock and I don't leave the office promptly at 5:00 P.M., so please don't criticize me if occasionally I take an extra few minutes."

He thought for a moment and said, "The problem is that when you stay longer so do the others."

I understood, and I tried to abide by the fifteen-minute rule. He never said anything further about it.

Bob Brody was a religious Jew. Often rabbis came to solicit for their Yeshivas (schools). No matter how I tried to stop the rabbis from walking past me, they ignored me and marched into his office. While he told them he had no money, eventually he wrote a check. They never walked out empty handed.

Bob Brody, a lifelong heavy smoker, was probably in his sixties when he was diagnosed with cancer of the esophagus. He suffered terribly over a long period of time. He was repeatedly hospitalized while the doctors stretched his esophagus. I visited him in the hospital and brought him a new bow tie. Bow ties were his signature. On his first day back to the office, he wore that tie. It was his way of thanking me and I appreciated his thoughtfulness.

Business had to go on as usual. During his hospital stays, he would call and ask me to come to his bedside and take some dictation. I would grab my steno pad and take a cab to Northwestern Hospital. As sick as he was, he still dictated fast and furiously. By this time I had worked for him long enough that he knew he could trust me to sign his letters and mail them out.

As Bob became evermore ill, the junior partner participated more actively in the management of the office. I tried but was unable to work with him. He changed all the rules. The things that I used to do routinely now had to be approved by him. He ranted and raved at everybody, including his wife over the telephone. I had been with this firm for nine years, but I knew under the circumstances I could not stay. I began to look for another job. Since Bob Brody was still alive, I felt guilty leaving him while he was so sick.

Shortly after I left, I attended his funeral.

I might have stayed with Brody & Gore for the rest of my working life if it had not been for the untimely demise of both senior partners. After working there for many years, our relationship had grown to one of mutual trust, respect, and even friendship.

CHAPTER XV
DANNY'S ILLNESS INTENSIFIES

While I worked at Brody & Gore, Danny's illness consumed him more and more and he was able to work less and less. He frequently called me at the office. My friend Lois often intercepted his calls, telling him I was unavailable. He traveled all over the country in order to get away from his paranoia, while the children and I were truly struggling. Clearly, it was his illness that kept him from supporting the children and the voices in his head dictated his behavior. I knew I had to act when I received a letter from Las Vegas stating that he was unable to send any child support because, "While one prostitute was on me the other one went through my pockets and stole my money."

Anger welled up in my heart and the children's needs superseded my sympathy for Danny. I turned to one of the attorneys at my office for help. Mr. Dennen, who had many more years of practice behind him than ahead of him, went to court on my behalf on a rule to show cause, a court procedure requiring the appearance of the defendant. When Danny did not appear for the hearing, a warrant was issued for his arrest. Consequently, he was arrested and went to jail. I didn't want him in jail. He didn't belong in jail. I just needed the money for my family. We settled several thousand dollars worth of arrearage for $1,000, which his mother paid. The emotional damage this incident caused my children was not worth the money I received.

A young, divorced attorney at the firm befriended me and encouraged me to attend some singles functions to make a social life for myself. He even furnished me with the names of several singles organizations. Singles clubs were a real education. They consisted mostly of extremely bitter women who told stories about their cheating exes. Until then, I thought such stories only existed in cheap novels. The men in the group were at the bottom of the socioeconomic ladder. I used to refer to them as "factory rejects." Generally, men took it for granted that the husbands left the wives. I got very angry when men repeatedly asked, "How could your husband leave a lovely lady like you?"

Why did strangers assume my husband cheated on me and left me? I was not about to explain the story of my life just to make light conversation. It was none of their business.

My children looked over and scrutinized my first date as if he were ET from outer space. I don't even remember his name, and we never saw each other again. No matter, it lifted my spirits to know that I was still attractive enough to catch a man's eye. Besides being a mother, there was still a young woman lurking inside me.

I joined Parents Without Partners (PWP), a singles organization. Participation in their programs did not come easily. First, I hid in the kitchen, fixed coffee and helped with the refreshments. I made a few friends who urged me to take part in various activities. Some of their programs were specifically designed for children and their single parent. My children had an opportunity to meet others in similar one-parent situations. PWP also had adult activities. Soon I became a board member. I planned dances, dinners and family outings. I enjoyed this position and pretty soon I was the "Hostess with the Mostest." I became much more outgoing and at ease in social situations as well as in front of the microphone. I dated some of the men, but I never met anyone I would even consider marrying. Besides, I had made up my mind when I became single that I would under no circumstances bring a man into my house while the children lived at home. They had suffered enough. They were high priority. Not that there was much cause for concern; no one was knocking down the door to marry a woman with three young children.

As much as I tried to prolong it, selling my house became inevitable. The neighborhood totally changed. Violence became prevalent. We remained the only white family on the block. I knew we had to move when my daughter was afraid to walk out of the house after school. Selling the house was almost as traumatic as going through my divorce again. That house held many heartwarming memories of a happy family life, watching three children develop and grow. It also bore the scars of the breakup of a family. That was an overwhelming decision.

I started to look for a new home. At first, I contemplated moving further south to the suburbs, but my children wanted to go north where most of their friends had moved. The problem was that property in the northern suburbs was considerably more expensive. I spent every weekend looking for an affordable and suitable home for my children, a dog, two cats and me. It was a package deal, all or nothing. I saw some two-bedroom townhouses with finished basements that were within my means. I considered turning the basement into a room for my boys. We would have been crowded. Then, a realtor showed me a three-bedroom, bath-and-a-half co-op apartment that the owner was willing to sell on contract. The private basement with laundry facilities was a bonus. I knew I didn't need to look any further. In March 1971, we moved into our new home at 8300 Christiana in Skokie and lived there for fifteen years.

Once again, I was blessed with kind and caring neighbors, Al and Roz Fleigel and their two young adult children, Kelly and Adrienne. Knowing I was a single mother with young ones, they looked after my children and me as if we were part of their family. Adrienne's new looking hand-me-downs provided a chic office wardrobe for me. Al worked downtown. Year after year, he drove me to work on a daily basis. Now, Al and Roz are both gone, but Adrienne and I maintain a warm relationship. In 1981, after my youngest child married, I remarried and moved into my new husband's condo. My previous residence became rental property until it sold in September 2008.

My former employers, Brody & Gore, were very good to me. They handled my legal problems regarding child support, the sale of my home, the purchase of the apartment, and never charged me a penny. May they rest in peace.

CHAPTER XVI
BLOOD MONEY

While working at Brody and Gore, I received a letter from Gabriella, my father's widow, telling me that my father had applied for restitution from the German government. He left half of the proceeds to her and the other half to me. In order for her to collect her share, I had to sign off on it. I had to make a personal appearance at the German Consulate on Michigan Avenue to receive approximately $400. To walk into the German Consulate was a very emotional ordeal. I had not been that frightened since I arrived in the United States. While nobody appeared threatening, I had a feeling of being suffocated. I felt as if a rock was sitting on my chest; I could hardly breathe. It is impossible to describe the panic and fear that engulfed me. My blood pressure must have gone off the charts. The money was to be compensation for my mother's fur coat and jewelry. To the Germans, evidently her life wasn't worth anything. How dare you! I wanted to say, "Don't insult me with your $400. You can have your money, her jewelry and fur coat, just give me back my mother." After I stepped outside I took a deep breath. Once again, God bless the U.S.A.

CHAPTER XVII
FORGOTTEN AND LONELY

During the tumultuous years while I was raising three children by myself, my cousin Paul and his wife Jackie, as well as my cousin Tom, settled in California. Uncle Eugene retired. Aunt Betsy and Uncle Eugene missed their children and wanted to enjoy their grandchildren. There was nothing to keep them in Chicago. As they aged, Chicago's bitter cold winters became difficult to tolerate. They sold their condominium on Lake Shore Drive and moved to Los Angeles. There was little communication between us. They didn't even remember my children's birthdays. My cousins were busy carving out their careers and raising their families. I seldom heard from them. On my birthday and at Christmas, I received a card with a small gift from my uncle and aunt. An occasional phone call and a word of empathy and encouragement now and then would have gone a long way. What happened to my children and me could have happened to anyone. Schizophrenia could strike anyone, rich or poor. I did not look for this problem. It fell upon me with a crushing blow. There was no one to lift even a feather off my shoulder.

Where was this family I was supposed to be a part of? Was I ever really a part of the Kuhn family? It was easier for them to watch their boys succeed and bask in the joy of seeing their grandchildren grow. I felt totally alone and forgotten.

CHAPTER XVIII
STEPPING UP THE LADDER

Once I made the decision to leave Brody & Gore, I very quickly found a job as secretary/office manager at a small firm. This position paid as much for working five days a week as I had been receiving for five-and-a-half days. This attorney wanted me so badly he was willing to waive the waiting period for health insurance and other benefits and offered me a three-week vacation the first year. This also was a litigation firm. Brody & Gore primarily practiced insurance defense law, while this firm represented plaintiffs. At my new job, I had an opportunity to utilize my training in bookkeeping. I did the payroll and paid the bills. My boss praised me and told me I would have a job with him until we were both ready to retire. This was true until we needed additional personnel and I hired Joan, an extremely capable young woman who worked for much less than I did. Life taught me another bitter lesson: you don't hire anyone who is capable of walking in your shoes. While Joan could not do the bookkeeping or payroll, she could do enough to make herself very valuable. I had been with this employer for approximately two years when he told me that there was no future for me with him. It was clear that I needed to move on.

With each job I had learned something new and my skills had become more diversified. Once again I was looking through the Law Bulletin in search of employment. Evidently I interviewed well because I never had any problem finding a position. Almost immediately, I accepted a job offer with another small litigation firm. My new employer was a miser and a slave driver. He came alive at 5:00 P.M., when I was ready to go home. He expected me to work until all hours of the night without any extra pay. After doing the work of two for a year, I asked for a raise. When he turned me down, I knew it was time to move on. I sent out résumés in answer to some blind ads. I must have sent a résumé to one of his friends because he came back from court one day and asked, "Did you find a job yet?"

He had put me in the awkward position of having to leave as soon as possible instead of having the luxury of finding the job I really wanted.

CHAPTER XIX
ESTATE PLANNING LAW FIRM

I interviewed for the position of secretary to the senior partner at a firm with approximately 30 attorneys. My boss was a soft-spoken, pleasant man. With his salt and pepper hair, he looked impressive in his blue pinstriped suit. He was married, had two grown children and several grandchildren. I loved the way he spoke of his wife, calling her his bride. His specialty was estate planning, wills and trusts. Here I had a chance to learn about another aspect of the practice of law. This specialty was not as interesting as litigation, but it added to my bank of knowledge.

I had worked for this attorney for about two-and-a-half years when around Christmas in 1980, the office manager called me in and informed me that my boss felt "we didn't mesh." In essence, she fired me. I was heartbroken and could not understand why. I asked her what kind of references I might expect. She said, "The best." None of it made any sense. After I left the firm, my friend Betsy kept me apprised of the office gossip. Once I was gone, *Joe,* my ex-boss, tried several secretaries before he settled on the one he wanted, a girl about his daughter's age. He wanted her so much that he got her pregnant. He left his wife of many years, *his bride,* to marry this young woman. At last, I understood why we didn't "mesh." That eased my pain. Although Betsy now lives in New England, we have remained close friends over the years.

CHAPTER XX
A SHOCKING TELEPHONE CALL

In May 1980, while working for the estate planning firm, I received a telephone call from my former mother-in-law. I hadn't talked to her for years and I don't know how she knew my phone number. Sobbing she said, "I know you don't care, but Danny died yesterday. He was hit by a truck walking along a highway in Las Vegas, Nevada." The news devastated me. I was numb. How could she think that I didn't care? I had been divorced for fifteen years but I still loved him. Besides, he was the father of my children. I asked myself, "How do I tell my children their father died?" I knew the news would cause them indescribable pain. I left the office and headed for home. All three of my children were grown and on their own by this time. I called them and asked them to come over as soon as possible. We sat around the dining room table reliving the past while attempting to deal with the present. Grandma wanted to cremate his body and fly his ashes home. My boys insisted on seeing his body. They had to be sure it was their father. My children and I went to the funeral. We laid Danny to rest in the Kittay family plot. The divorce had caused so much bad blood and confusion between the Kittays and my little family that after the funeral my children and I went home, while the rest of them went their own way. We couldn't even mourn together.

The day after we buried Danny, his sister Frances called me and at last we talked. We got together and I finally had an opportunity to ask, "Where were you when we needed you?" She apologized and told me, "You are right. We should have been there for you." While I accepted her apology, this was too little too late. My sons were her nephews and my daughter was her niece. She had turned her back on them, never remembered them. During his travels, Danny had gone to New York and stayed with Frances and her husband Gene. She knew how sick her brother was. Since we reconciled after the funeral, whenever Fran and Gene come to Chicago, we usually get together and visit the graves. We've remained friendly, but not close. We call each other occasionally, especially when there is illness in the family. As we age, poor health befalls us more often. My mother-in-law passed away in 1990 after a long bout with vascular disease. I tried to get my boys to visit her in the hospital, but they chose not to go. I didn't want them to regret not saying goodbye to her. They were adults. I could not and would not insist that they visit.

CHAPTER XXI
FINDING DR. COWAN

Over the years, I often thought about Dr. Cowan, the psychiatrist who initially treated Danny. I looked in the Yellow Pages for several years to see if I could find his name. He had shown great concern for my family and me when Danny was his patient. I just wanted to let him know that the children and I were doing all right and thank him for his kind support. Despite my efforts, I was unable to locate him.

In 2003, a few friends from our camping days contacted me. They were very enthusiastically planning a reunion and asked whether I would care to participate. I was very intrigued at the thought of renewing old acquaintances and I became deeply involved in the planning. As I scanned through a list of former campers, I came across a name from my past. Ned Cowan. Could this be the Dr. Ned Cowan I had searched for over the years? I asked my friend Alice, a psychiatric social worker, if she remembered him.

Alice, said, "Of course I remember him, Neddie became a psychiatrist."

He and his twin brother were campers after I got married. Unbelievable! I finally had found Dr. Ned Cowan. He had a California address. I wrote him and explained how I had been looking for him over the years just to say thank you and to let him know that my children and I had made a life for ourselves.

Upon receipt of my letter, he called me. We had a long conversation. He wasn't sure whether he remembered me, but he certainly remembered Danny. I learned that both my cousins, Paul and Tom, were his camp counselors. I looked forward to seeing him at the reunion, but he was unable to attend. What a bizarre development in my strange life. My search was over. Now I could close this chapter of my life and tuck it away in my heart.

CHAPTER XXII
MY NEXT AND FINAL JOB

In 1980, I met Henry Schwartz. We were planning to be married in February 1981. I had recently lost my job and didn't plan on looking for work until I returned from my honeymoon in the middle of March. However, after working steadily for many years, I got bored and restless and started looking at the want ads. In pursuit of a job, I met Bill Sneckenberg, a partner in the law firm of Lev and Sneckenberg. Bill was a tall, lean man with lots of blond hair and a mustache. He was more than ten years younger than I was. At our first meeting Bill offered me a very appealing job. It was a small office, totally in chaos, just waiting for me to put my organizational skills to work. I explained that I was planning to be married, going on my honeymoon, and it would be six weeks before I could start. Bill said, "I'll wait for you," and the rest of my working life was sealed with a handshake. For the first time, my new employer was younger than I was. I wondered if the age difference might become a problem.

The job was challenging, but I loved it. This was "my office," and I ran it the way I saw fit. I put all my energy into it as if it were my own business. Bill quickly became very dependent on me. He would say, "All I need is my buzzer and Agnes." He knew he could count on me. The firm specialized in Appellate Court work and I became well versed in editing and putting together documents for the Appellate Court. Many times I arrived at the crack of dawn or stayed until midnight when a deadline had to be met. I didn't mind a bit. The work was interesting and exciting. To watch a lawsuit grow from the beginning through the end of a trial was thrilling. Sometimes I slipped out of the office and went to court to watch Bill argue his case. It was agonizing to wait for a jury to return a verdict. Following a win, we celebrated. After listening to one of Bill's brilliant closing arguments, I told him, "You missed your calling, you should have been a Shakespearian actor." Before I left for vacation, I prepared all foreseeable documents to avoid any glitches while I was gone. Unless we were on a cruise, I kept in touch with the office and solved any small problems that arose. I loved my job. For the first time in my life, I was in a position to do as I pleased without worrying that my children might starve. It gave me a fantastic feeling of independence.

After the partnership of Lev and Sneckenberg dissolved, I stayed with Bill Sneckenberg for seventeen years before I retired. During my stay, I learned a great deal. It was a time of change for most workplaces. Computers had become a necessity. Bill, my boss, was very reluctant to become part of the electronic age. First he told me to buy something with memory, but no screen. Fortunately, I was familiar with memory typewriters and mag card machines, the precursors of computers. By the time he was willing to buy some PC's, we couldn't even give the mag card machines away. There were a couple of office moves and many personnel changes. I am proud of my record of interviewing and choosing prospective secretaries. Those I recommended for hire usually worked out well and stayed on the job for many years.

Bill met Kathleen, fell in love and got engaged. My husband Henry and I threw a lavish Sunday champagne brunch for them in our home. As the years went by, I watched their two babies come into the world and grow into lovely young ladies. I also saw many law clerks become fine attorneys. They were my "office children." I have remained friendly with several over the years. Ben Alba is currently a law professor at DePaul University's Law School. I learned a great deal from Ben about writing. Stuart Brody, Steve Thompson and Bill Sneckenberg formed a successful partnership. Renata Szczygiel married Ed Seward, another attorney, and they created the partnership of Seward & Szczygiel, PC. Louise Bauer practices family law. They are just a few of the fine young men and women who crossed my path over the years.

Bill and Kathleen honored me with an unforgettable, elegant retirement party at the Evanston Golf Club.

It has been more than ten years since I stopped working, but we stay in touch. I have a standing invitation to their annual Christmas party. Christine and Caroline, the Sneckenberg children, have grown into young adults. I was shocked when I heard that Christine, their eldest, had a brain tumor. She is now on the road to recovery. Christine is the same age as my granddaughter Ashley. My heartfelt best wishes for a total recovery are with her and her family.

FRONT ROW, LEFT TO RIGHT:

GRANDPA, holding Paul, Aunt Betsy's baby
Elza, holding me,
Grandma, Grandma's brother-in-law (husband of Janka), Janka on far
right.

BACK ROW, LEFT TO RIGHT:

Karcsi (Elza's husband), Betsy (Paul's Mother), my Father (Jenő) and
my Mother (Margit)

My Mother and I

My Mother

My Father

SECTION TWO
MY CHILDREN, MY DIAMONDS

CHAPTER I
MY FIRST BORN, STEVEN

Steven arrived on January 12, 1953, in Houston's recently completed New Methodist Hospital. He tipped the scale at eight pounds, six ounces. It cost us $10 a day out-of-pocket for a private room. In semi-private rooms, visiting hours were limited. In a private room, Danny could pop in anytime he was in the neighborhood. I stayed in the hospital for three days. The day I was discharged was one of the coldest days in Houston's history. The city is known for its hot and humid climate. Since they rarely had cold spells, homes were not built to withstand penetrating chill and dampness. Space heaters were the only source of heat, and the cold permeated every bone of my body.

Aunt Betsy came to help and show me how to care for a baby. I wanted to nurse my child but was unable to do so. I became ill and ran a high fever. I collapsed every time I attempted to stand up. My aunt took full charge of the baby and the household until I regained my strength. That's when she said, "Now I know why God gives babies to young people." I didn't realize the wisdom of that statement until many years later. After my aunt left, Grandma Kittay, my mother-in-law, came to meet her first grandchild and help with his care.

Seven months later, we returned to Chicago from Houston. After a brief stay with my in-laws, we moved into our own apartment, Steve and I took daily walks. I pushed him in an old fashioned pram as I shopped for groceries and ran errands while he slept. He had to have his daily airing. I thoroughly enjoyed taking care of my baby. I taught him nursery rhymes and read his favorite stories many times over until he could recite them.

In September 1957, my neighbor Marie brought my screaming four-year-old son to my door. While playing outside, he poked around a fire with a stick and the bottom of his pants ignited. Thank God my neighbor heard him scream and ran out to smother the flames with a blanket. By that time, Steve had sustained second and third degree burns on the lower quarter of his leg. It was the beginning of a nightmare.

My mother-in-law was very upset. She told me, "Anybody can have a baby, but not everybody is capable of caring for one."

Ouch, that hurt. I was upset enough about my child's injuries; I didn't need her nasty comment. She was very attached to Steve, her first grandchild. Probably, that's why she uttered those spiteful words.

Besides Steve, I had a toddler, my thirteen-month-old son Billy, and my newborn daughter Cheryl to occupy my attention.

My precious little Steve suffered terribly. The gauze stuck to the open wound and every change of dressing subjected him to great pain and anguish. We kept waiting for the wound to heal, but it didn't. Because he was constantly losing bodily fluids through the open wound, we were very concerned about the possibility of a serious infection. He lost weight and became anemic and pale. His injuries were clearly sapping his energy and immune system. We went from doctor to doctor, but to no avail. After waiting for several months for the burn to heal, our pediatrician suggested we consult a plastic surgeon to see if a skin graft might be the solution. Subsequently, Steve was admitted to Sarah Morris, the children's wing at Michael Reese Hospital. Doctor Richter, a plastic surgeon transplanted a layer of skin from his thigh to the burned area. The surgery was successful and Steve was finally on the mend.

My son shared a hospital room with another blond little boy. I didn't know what was wrong with the other child. One day, as I walked into his room I saw a little blond head sticking out from under the sheet. The other bed was empty. My heart stopped. Obviously, the sheet was pulled over a dead body. I let out a scream that could have been heard across the ocean. The nurses came running, apologizing profusely, explaining that the other child had died. They had moved Steve to another room. My heart raced, blood rushed to my brain as I came close to becoming a patient myself.

Steve made a quick and full recovery after his surgery. We regretted we didn't have this procedure done sooner, but we had hoped that his wounds would heal without subjecting him to an operation. He was now old enough for kindergarten. Unfortunately, his immune system became compromised as a result of the burn and surgery. Once he started school and came into contact with other children, he was susceptible to every virus and infection. Whenever Steve got sick, his two younger siblings also got sick. Our pediatrician was a constant visitor at our home. Doctors made house calls those days; nobody took a feverish child to the doctor. Plastic disposable syringes had not yet been invented. I boiled many needles and syringes in a small pot of water to sterilize them so the doctor could inject penicillin into my ailing children.

In the spring of 1958, on the recommendation of our pediatrician, we took Steve out of school for the first semester of kindergarten. After a summer of playing in the sun, his system rebounded. His physical scars faded with time; the emotional scars still remain. Even now, he finds it difficult to walk into a hospital and gets upset at the sight of a hypodermic needle or a drop of blood.

When he was six years old, Steve came down with the chicken pox just before Christmas. He was very worried that Santa Claus might not come to a house with chicken pox. We assured him that Santa was immune to the chicken pox and would not stay away because he was sick. I didn't count on catching it from him. Many childhood diseases had escaped me while I was young. I had the measles when I was sixteen and caught the chicken pox and mumps from my children. Of course, my two younger children had chicken pox along with me. It was difficult for Santa to complete her shopping, but the children were not disappointed.

Show and tell was one of the highlights of kindergarten, and Steve told his class, "Mommy got so much perfume for the holidays that she will never have to take a bath again."

Steve loved baseball and we signed him up to play Little League. He was tall and husky, and when he connected, the ball went high over the fence, but heaven help the team if he had to run the bases. The first year he played, his team made it into the Little League World Series. It was exciting for the whole family. The season culminated in a banquet celebrating his team's winning record. Steve's Little League career continued until he became a teenager.

While Steve was in high school in the 60's, I got a call that the principal wanted to see me. This was a command, not an invitation. What sin had my son committed? Horrors! He went to school in cutoffs and sandals without wearing socks. For that I had to take time off from work to talk to the principal. It really seems funny when today's students not only dress as they please but tote guns to school. Now even teachers wear flip-flops and jeans.

Steve came home from high school one day, looking very sheepish. I asked, "What's wrong?"

He carefully weighed his words and then blurted out, "Linda (his girl friend) and I cut school today. We were on the train going downtown and we met Grandma."

I asked, "How did you explain this to Grandma?"

"I told her we were going to the museum on a school field trip." He then added, "Please Mom, don't tell Grandma."

I scolded him but I never did tell.

At one time Steve had two paper routes, one in the morning and the other in the afternoon. I begged him, "Please give up either the morning or the afternoon route."

He answered, "I will give one up after I get my Christmas tips." And he did.

Steve is a born businessman. From the time he was old enough to deliver newspapers, he held some kind of job. In high school, I never had to give him any spending money or buy him clothes. Since money was scarce, his ability to take care of his own needs was an enormous help. His emotional support and his grasp of Danny's illness were very comforting to me. After learning to drive, he paid the car insurance premiums. Steve was the only one of my children old enough to understand the nature of his father's illness and what it was doing to our family. I regret that he was cheated out of his childhood.

On frigid Sunday mornings, I drove him around on his paper route. This became a very special time for us. It gave us a chance to talk heart to heart. With all that was happening at home, there was much to discuss. Steve was a big boy and looked older than his years. At age fifteen, he went to work for Jewel Supermarket. He stayed with Jewel through high school and college. After graduating from the University of Illinois, Jewel offered him a permanent position and wanted to enroll him in their management training program. Steve chose to leave and went to work for another food purveyor, Scandia Foods, where eventually he became Sales Manager.

We were all very surprised when in 1987, after having worked in the food industry all his life, Steve announced, "I am going into the printing business." He started Creekside Printing in Rolling Meadows with a one-room office. His business grew until it swallowed up all the space in the building. He is a workaholic, but I really think he enjoys it. Before he relocated his business to Elgin in 1988, the Rolling Meadows Chamber of Commerce honored him as "Merchant of the year." We proudly attended the banquet. Unfortunately, with the advent of the computer and current economic times, it is a struggle to keep a printing business going.

Steven, my special eldest child, I am very proud of you and I love you with all my heart.

CHAPTER II
MY MIDDLE CHILD, BILLY

When Steve was about two, while attending a wedding in New York, I suffered a miscarriage. However, within a few months, I was pregnant again. This pregnancy was much easier. Billy arrived on August 18, 1956, weighing six pounds, eight ounces. He was a delicate, fair skinned platinum blond, but so tiny and fragile compared to Steve. Since I had become very ill and had a terrible experience trying to nurse my first child, I didn't even try with the second. I regret that decision. I think my milk would have agreed with him better than the formula. He was a very colicky infant and suffered from gas pains much longer than most babies.

Once again, Aunt Betsy came to stay with Steve while I was in the hospital and helped me after I got home. Grandma Kittay followed.

I felt Grandma favored Steve, and my heart went out to my little Billy who was so much smaller and quite sickly, often plagued with diarrhea and colds. I really believe he was allergic to the formula and later on to milk.

Billy was a bright, nimble baby who quickly learned to crawl. By the time he was ten months old he was walking and trying to climb on the sofa. I had to keep a constant eye on him to keep him from hurting himself. My neighbor's young daughter Jordie had a doll buggy Billy loved to push. Actually, he pushed Jordie aside so he could have the buggy. We bought him a little red wagon thinking it might replace the buggy. The children resolved the conflict: Jordie played with the wagon while Billy pushed the buggy.

Billy had a favorite panda bear that went everywhere with him. I surgically repaired "Pandy" many times. He was a very affectionate child who loved to hug and kiss. That stopped when his older brother started to tease him about it.

During a visit to the pediatrician, I glanced at his chart. It read, "petite built." Billy may have looked petite, but he was a daredevil. We should have called him "Fearless Bill" because he was willing to try anything and everything to keep up with the older children on the block.

We became well known at South Chicago Hospital's emergency room. He had more stitches in his life than my other two children combined. Besides stitches, he fell onto the pavement from a grocery cart and his sister fell on top of him. That time, he broke his shoulder. He was cast in a Napoleon-like position all summer, which was hot and uncomfortable.

Then there was the "scissors" incident. Playing on the living room floor, Billy was cutting out pictures when I heard a scream. Blood spurted to the ceiling and all over the carpeting. The point of the scissors had gone into the artery at his wrist. It took a visit to the emergency room and one stitch to close the wound, and a lot of elbow grease to clean up the blood.

Billy enjoyed gardening, but was allergic to everything he touched in the yard. On a hot summer day, I put him down for a nap and when he awoke his entire face was swollen and distorted. The doctor said he must have handled something in the yard and then touched his face. I put him in the stroller and off we went to the corner drugstore for Benadryl.

Billy was a friendly, outgoing child. I thought kindergarten would be a simple adjustment for him, but not so. He was jealous of my time with his younger sister Cheryl and unhappy about leaving the two of us alone. One time when I took him into the classroom through one door, he ran out through the other door, with the janitor chasing him, afraid he might run in front of a car. Rather than dealing with an unruly child, Miss King, the kindergarten teacher, told me to take Billy home. Obviously, this was the easier route for her, but not the right thing for my son.

In first grade, Billy was under the watchful eyes of *Mrs. Robins* who looked and acted like a bulldog. She told me in no uncertain terms that she hated teaching first graders and complained about the terribly difficult job of trying to teach and keep order in a classroom of six-year olds. She constantly compared Billy to his older brother.

Unfortunately, this problem followed Billy through the rest of his school years. He had to find a niche between a bigger and more academically inclined older brother and a cute little sister. Billy was caught up in the middle-child syndrome. He was just as intelligent as his brother and as good looking as his baby sister, but the comparisons hurt him. He found his place in the family by acting out rather than competing with his siblings. Smaller than most children his age, he was very agile and extremely clever with his little hands. He got a standing ovation when he climbed the rope to the top of the gym at the JCC. Nobody else in his class could match this feat. Like his dad, he could fix anything and everything. When his dad's fingers were too large to reach a tiny screw, Billy came to the rescue and removed the screw with ease.

Billy was a toddler when his dad and Uncle Leo, Grandma's brother-in-law, attempted to assemble a sandbox on the patio. Billy watched intently. Uncle Leo mumbled under his breath, "I can't find that screw. Where did that screw go?"

Billy said, "Just a minute." He went into the house and returned with a screw.

His dad looked at him puzzled and asked, "Where did you get that?"

Billy amazed them with his answer: "I took it out of my bed." To him, playing in the sandbox was more important than sleeping.

In 1971, when Billy was in the eighth grade, we moved to Skokie. He still hated school. I thought the new environment at a different school might make a difference. The Skokie school system tried its best to interest him in various programs, but he did not want any part of it. He was a troubled teenager and I knew it, but I did not know how to help him. I received different advice from several professionals. Getting him out of bed and ready for school became a daily shouting match. Many times I did not succeed and had to leave the house in order to get to work. Somebody suggested I buy him an alarm clock and make him responsible for getting himself up and off to school. Of course, that did not work either. Finally, because of his truancy, I was summoned to appear in court. I still don't know how an experienced, caring therapist from the Jewish Children's Bureau heard of our plight. She came to my assistance so heaven forbid they would not put my child in the Audy Home for delinquents. I only remember the therapist as "Judy." We started family counseling with her. At the first session, she asked Billy, "Are you scared?"

He gave a blasé answer "Naw, I don't care."

Judy answered with one word, "Bullshit." That broke the ice. All my children were reluctant to attend, and it was next to impossible to get them to talk. Cheryl expressed her discomfort at the sessions by giggling in a very inappropriate manner.

It was Judy's recommendation that Billy be removed from the family and placed in a home, operated by the Jewish Children's Bureau, specifically designed for helping troubled teens. He was about sixteen at the time.

I had to make another huge decision all by myself. I knew I had lost control long ago. Would this place be better for him than home? If I agreed to this move, I also had to agree to allow him to remain there for a year. I finally decided that since I was unable to help him at home, I had to give Judy's recommendation a try. I signed the papers with a very heavy heart. The main reason I consented to this arrangement was that he would be compelled to attend school. It didn't work. His truancy continued. We saw each other often during that year, but he did not come back to live with us until the year was up.

I honestly don't think being out of our home helped him, but I don't think it hurt him either. When Billy moved back home, things remained status quo; he still didn't go to school. I kept telling myself that with time he would grow up, but growing up came very slowly and painfully.

One Saturday, while attempting to clean under his bed, I found a couple of books typically of interest to teenagers: *The Joys of Sex*, and *How to Grow Pot Under Artificial Lights*. It suddenly clicked. Mother, how dumb can you be! My son had a lovely green plant growing in his room under artificial lights. I chuckle now, but it certainly wasn't funny at the time. Bye bye plant. Into the garbage it went. While Billy didn't say anything, his facial expression reflected his shock at my quick no-nonsense attitude.

Early in his life, I singled out Billy as the child who needed my protection from the world. The more I felt his pain, the more I sheltered him. It became a vicious cycle. My biggest sin was that I loved him too much. Oh how I wish I could do it over! I certainly didn't do him any favors. It is much easier to see my mistakes in retrospect, but I cannot undo the past.

While growing up was a struggle for Billy, he ultimately carved out a career for himself in the hotel industry. He started at the bottom and eventually worked his way up to the position of Chief Engineer at some major hotel chains. Raising his son, Charles, as a single parent, was probably his greatest accomplishment. I take pride in having watched Billy grow from a troubled child into a very capable, warmhearted adult.

Billy, my special middle child, I am so proud of you and I love you with all my heart.

CHAPTER III
A NEW GENERATION ON THE HORIZON

In the spring of 1979, Billy announced, "I am getting married!"

"What?" I asked myself, did I hear right? My twenty-two-year-old son who never finished high school and never worked is now getting married?

Yes, it was true. Joyce, his high school sweetheart, was pregnant with his child. After I recovered from the shock, I welcomed Joyce with open arms and hoped that the responsibility of a family would be good for my son.

Joyce was the only child of Les and Judy Green. They had adopted her when she was an infant. The Greens invited us for dinner at their Park Ridge condo. Everything in their apartment sparkled. There were mirrors, crystals and diamonds everywhere. Both Les and Judy wore big diamond rings and their names were spelled out with diamonds on their gold bracelets. Their home glittered and glistened. This obviously was a nouveau-riche family. Les's love for his daughter was apparent. He doted on her and gave her anything and everything she desired. That included, fashionable clothes, a sporty car and lots of spending money. No young man could compete with the material things Les provided for her. I had the impression that despite his limited education, Les had amassed a fortune in the scrap metal business. The only thing Joyce lacked was love and affection from her mother. Judy was a very self-centered woman with no warmth and no heart. My friends threw bridal showers, while Les and Judy made a hasty wedding for the children. The ceremony took place in a Lincolnwood Synagogue and a sumptuous reception followed at the Greens' condo recreation room. My son seemed so happy! He promised to work hard to take care of his family. Les helped him get a truck, while Billy looked for odd jobs as a handyman.

Soon after the wedding, we learned that Les was terminally ill with cancer of the liver. This was very hard on Joyce; the twin strengths of her rock and pillar were crumbling. Les was in and out of the hospital, tormented with pain. Judy couldn't deal with her husband's illness and disappeared for long periods of time.

On October 18, 1979, the long-awaited telephone call came; my daughter-in-law, Joyce, was in labor. My first grandchild was about to be born. I left the office and headed for Lutheran General Hospital. I was filled with anticipation, hope and worry. My mind drifted back over the years and I could hear my mother-in-law say with the arrival of each grandchild, "Another one to worry about." When I was young, her statement was totally meaningless. Now, I understood. I wore out my shoes and the carpeting as I paced the floor all night in the waiting room. Billy, of course, was with Joyce. Judy came and went, saying, "There is nothing I can do here. I might as well go home and get some sleep." I was left alone with only my thoughts to keep me company.

On October 19, around four in the morning, Charles Benjamin came into the world. I watched the nurse wheel the little basket with this darling baby into the nursery. I found myself thinking: child of my child, you are a part of me. You are the most beautiful baby boy in the world. I could not hide, nor did I care to, the flood of emotions and awe that enveloped me.

The nurse smiled as she said, "This must be your first grandchild."

Suddenly, my life took on new meaning, and I knew why I had survived. God had granted me life while others perished so that I could procreate. I did not anticipate the difficulties that lay ahead for both my son and grandson. For now, it was time to rejoice and celebrate.

Shortly after Charles's birth, we buried Les, Joyce's father. Judy, my son's mother-in-law, did not miss an opportunity to urge her daughter to file for a divorce and find the husband she deserved, a husband better able to provide for her. She even repeated this to my boss while they were both guests at my daughter's wedding. Joyce's life was falling apart too. She could no longer ask her Daddy for money. Her mother would give her nothing, either financially or emotionally.

I will never forget Billy proudly stating, "This baby will have a father" as he walked around singing, "We are family." Although it did my heart good to see him so happy, there were major financial problems. Billy and his family came to live with me for a while. However, that didn't alleviate their troubles. I watched Joyce give the baby a bottle while she read a book. She, like her mother, lacked the basic warmth to nurture a child.

Before her pregnancy, Joyce talked about becoming a dental hygienist. Her father had left some money earmarked for her education. She applied and was admitted into Northwestern University's Dental Hygienist Program and eventually received her degree. Before long, she filed for divorce and put the baby in day care. Billy was crushed. He loved his child and I loved them both, but there was nothing I could do to help. I looked in the mirror and asked, "Is history repeating itself? Will the lives of my children be patterned after mine?"

An imaginary snowball started to form on top of a hill, making its way slowly down the slope.

CHAPTER IV
MY BABY GIRL, CHERYL

On September 3, 1957, a year and two weeks after Billy was born, my precious daughter Cheryl arrived, weighing seven pounds, eleven ounces. The doctor warned me to go to the hospital at the first sign of labor because third babies have a tendency to come quickly. He was right. I almost gave birth on the hospital steps. Compared to my previous pregnancies, this was an easy delivery. They took me directly into the delivery room, where Cheryl made her appearance during the wee hours of the morning. She was in a hurry to leave the comfort of my womb and face the world. My doctor was buttoning his shirt as he sprinted into the delivery room. I was wide awake during her birth and had the pleasure of holding my newborn on my belly even before the cord was cut. Only another woman with a similar experience could understand the feeling of contentment and bliss of holding and feeling a newborn.

Once again, my aunt came to care for my two older children while I was in the hospital. Grandma helped after I brought the baby home.

Cheryl was born with thick dark hair that soon was replaced by lovely blonde curls. I had my precious little girl. With two boys and a girl, my family was complete. Cheryl seldom cried. She nursed and slept as if she knew there were two other children in the house who needed my attention. I was already selecting colorful ribbons for her hair to match each outfit.

Having two babies a year apart was difficult, especially the first year. There were two sets of diapers and two sets of bottles to juggle. I had a great helper, an elderly black lady, Josephine Kirk. She truly loved my children, and they loved her. But their efforts to say, "Josephine" turned into "Yaya." For the rest of her life, to us she remained "Yaya." The day we moved into our new house, she took my three children home with her to get them away from the tumult of moving. I trusted her implicitly. She helped me and babysat for us for many years. I can still see her standing Billy on top of the washing machine saying, "Billy, repeat after me and say your speech." With that she held his little arms up above his head and recited: "Here I stand on two little chips, please come kiss my sweet little lips." She also nicknamed Cheryl "Putzy."

Soon after Cheryl's first birthday, we moved into our new home at 9205 South Chappel. I tried a new spring coat and bonnet on her. She looked adorable and I wanted to take her picture. She was just over a year old and not very steady on her feet. I told her to sit on the back porch while I ran into the house to get my camera. I was gone only a few seconds, but when I got back, Cheryl was gone. I panicked and ran around screaming her name. I found her at a little convenience store across the street. Miraculously, she crossed a busy street without getting hit by a car. Because of her little adventure, we promptly installed a fence.

During the preschool years, Billy and Cheryl were companionable, almost like twins. One day, as they were playing in Cheryl's room behind closed doors, my motherly intuition told me it was too quiet and I'd better check it out. As I opened the door, to my horror, I saw a campfire built out of old newspapers in the middle of the room. The frilly bedspread and curtains were inches from the flames. I was grateful nobody had been hurt. The flooring was ruined, but that could be replaced, a small problem compared to the gravity of the disaster that thankfully had been averted. Little boys love to play with matches. I had already told my two younger ones about Steve's painful accident, but that didn't seem to deter them. I had to keep the matches hidden.

Unlike her brother Billy, Cheryl was quiet, reserved and slow to warm up to strangers. The following year, she started kindergarten. My shy little girl took to school immediately.

One day when Cheryl came home from school, she showed me a picture she drew of our cat. We sat together while she had some milk and cookies and rambled on about her day's activities. My ears perked up as she said, "Judy told me you speak with an accent.'"

Cheryl answered her, "What accent? My mommy has no accent."

I laughed. Of course she didn't hear her mommy's accent. She grew up with it and didn't know the difference.

When Cheryl was about ten, I was working at Wilson & Co., when she called me crying hysterically. At this office, the desks were in very close proximity to each other. It was very difficult to have a private telephone conversation. Cheryl, cried, "Mommy, it bit me. It bit me. I am going to get rabies and I will die."

"What bit you?" I asked.

"The rat, it bit me." At home, among many other creatures, we had a white rat with beady red eyes that lived in a cage. In a whisper I explained that even though rats can carry rabies, this rat had never been out of a cage and never had the opportunity to be infected. I said, "Wash the bite with soap and water and put some hydrogen peroxide on it." My daughter survived the bite, and so did I.

For a while, we had a menagerie: a dog, two cats, a white rat, some gerbils, and a goldfish. Eventually, the cats eliminated the gerbils. We gave the rat away to one of Billy's friends who had a Great Dane. The Great Dane ate the white rat with the red beady eyes, and the goldfish died of natural causes. We enjoyed the dog and the two cats for many years; these animals were best pals. They looked after and took care of each other. When I walked the dog, the cats walked along. People used to marvel at them.

Cheryl was almost ready to graduate from middle school when we moved into our apartment in Skokie. She had no problem making friends in her new surroundings. Once she started at Niles East High School, her social circle consisted of all Gentiles. Her lack of Jewish friends disturbed me. She was very self-conscious of her crooked teeth. I knew she needed braces. Cheryl was a chubby child. As she became a teenager, being overweight obviously bothered her. After completing her freshman year, Cheryl lost her baby fat and returned to school in the fall as a svelte, well-groomed young lady. Her thick blonde hair and large sparkling eyes were always her assets. As the pounds melted away, the breasts I never knew she had emerged. She also had a waistline. Almost overnight, she developed into a very shapely, pretty young lady. We shopped for new clothes to accentuate her new figure. When she returned to school in the fall, her friends hardly recognized her.

My cousin Bernice and her husband Oscar referred us to the orthodontist who had straightened their children's teeth. We made an appointment for a consultation. He mapped out his plan for treatment and we discussed his fee. I explained that I was raising three children as a single mother and needed a payment plan I could afford. He allowed me three years to fully pay him instead of the usual two. He did a superb job on my daughter's teeth. She still receives compliments on her smile.

Cheryl was still Mama's girl, and I had visions that she might be inclined to stay home with me for the rest of her life. I feared her goal might be to become my companion and my caretaker. That was not the life I wanted for her. She really surprised me when she started to talk about going away to college. I thought to myself, it sure would be great for her to have an opportunity to go away to school, but how could I possibly manage it financially? Where will this money come from?

She applied to several universities. We filled out forms for scholarships, grants and loans. There were too many forms even to count. It was easier to obtain scholarships then than it is today, and she did get them. She was accepted to the University of Illinois at Champaign-Urbana. As a result of her father's disability, she received a small monthly check from the Social Security Administration. That check became her spending money. I took on a second job typing reports at home.

Cheryl always loved babies and small children and she majored in early childhood development. When she became a sophomore, much against my wishes, she joined a sorority where she was the only Jewish girl. She made no secret of being Jewish, she lit Hanukah candles for the girls in her sorority house. She turned into a social butterfly.

During her junior year, Cheryl met John Hymel. John and Cheryl graduated from the University of Illinois at the same time. After graduation, my family met John's mother, father and two sisters. We dined together to celebrate this important milestone in our children's lives.

CHAPTER V
CHERYL AND JOHN

John became a frequent visitor at our house. Clearly, this was a serious romance. John earned his Bachelor's degree in computer science. Illinois Bell offered him a position, which he accepted. Cheryl was offered a position in Orange County, California. Her career goal was to become a Child Life Specialist. She decided to forego that offer in order that John could accept his position with Illinois Bell. Instead, she took a job at St. Francis Hospital in Evanston. Within a short time, it became obvious that John's family, especially his mother, did not approve of this romance. John had been raised in the Lutheran faith and we were Jewish. The following summer, John gave Cheryl an engagement ring.

I waited for John's mother to call. When days passed and I didn't hear from her, I picked up the phone and called her and said, "Congratulations." The telephone went dead in my ear. She did not hang up; she was just silent. Obviously, she was against this marriage. That was my initiation into the Hymel family.

For the children's sake, I felt we must make every effort to get along. Since Cheryl's birthday is around Labor Day, I invited John's mother, father and two younger sisters for a combined birthday and engagement celebration. My daughter and I cleaned, shopped, cooked, and set the table with great care. Nobody showed up. At the last minute Mrs. Hymel called and feigned illness. John was already at my house. My heart bled for him. He was caught in the middle.

The wedding was planned for the following summer. It was a very stressful time for Cheryl. She tried very hard to win over the Hymel family but was unsuccessful. She asked John's two sisters to be junior bridesmaids, but their mother vetoed it. My friends and Cheryl's, threw elaborate bridal showers. The young couple received lovely, useful gifts for their new home. The rehearsal dinner was painfully silent. On Cheryl's wedding day, John's mother showed her disdain for her new daughter-in-law by not talking to her. Cheryl kept saying, "It doesn't matter," but I knew better.

The wedding took place on July 13, 1980 at Fontana D'Or, an elegant banquet hall on Grand Avenue in Chicago. They specialize in weddings, large and small. We had chosen a luncheon wedding since it was less costly than a dinner. Waiters in black tuxedos and white gloves served the guests. Cheryl wore a bridal gown made of satin and lace. It had long, see-through sleeves, a standup neckline that came to a vee and a long train that tied into a bustle after the ceremony. Tiny pearls adorned the gown and matching veil. My daughter looked exquisite. I was bursting with pride. The color scheme was green and peach. The floral centerpieces, with a touch of peach, complemented the bridesmaids' green dresses. I wore a long beige gown. The men in the wedding party wore tuxedos. Steve walked his sister down the aisle and Billy was an usher. My daughter-in-law Joyce was invited to be matron of honor, but she declined. My friend, a Unitarian Minister, performed the nonsectarian ceremony. We had about 120 guests. I was disappointed that my uncle and aunt were unable to attend because Uncle Eugene had suffered an injury to his back.

Cheryl and John were saving their money to pay for the wedding. For many years, I continued to pay the premiums on a small life insurance policy on Danny. With the money I received from the insurance company upon his death, I was able to spruce up the wedding. Besides the three-tiered wedding cake, we had a sweet table that overflowed with cakes, pies, ice cream and various fruits. The guests danced while the band played. My daughter had the wedding I wished I could have had.

The children bought a duplex in Bartlett and settled into their new home. Cheryl worked at a travel agency. She was not looking for a career. Her goal was raising a family. They appeared to be very happy.

I was thrilled when I heard Cheryl was expecting. While her pregnancy was difficult, the delivery of Jonathan Daniel appeared to be relatively simple. I had hoped that the arrival of a grandchild would bring the two families together. I guess it was too much to expect. Towards the end of the pregnancy, John put his name on a list at Illinois Bell for a possible transfer to Florida. Although he didn't think he would be selected, he was.

While I was upset by their move, I felt that living a thousand miles from her mother-in-law would benefit the marriage. I spent a week with Cheryl helping her with her new baby Jonathan, who looked exactly like his father. Soon they packed up their belongings and moved to Florida.

Cheryl and John bought a home in Orlando, and Adam and Ashley were born there. After Ashley came into the world, Cheryl and the family moved into a larger, newly built, more spacious four-bedroom house with a big screened in porch, two cars in the garage and a perfect spot for a swimming pool. I tried to visit twice a year and always came home with the impression that this was a good, solid marriage. Several years in a row, my second husband Henry and I babysat while John and Cheryl vacationed. It was quality time with my grandchildren. I was very happy for my daughter. She had everything I hadn't had when I was her age. This was my perfect family. I lived vicariously through her pleasures.

CHAPTER VI
BYE BYE HAPPY HOME

Henry and I were visiting in Florida the year Cheryl walked around slamming doors and yelling at everybody. Something was obviously very wrong. I finally took her aside and asked, "What's going on, what's wrong?"

She said, "I want a divorce!"

I was so shocked I could barely speak. I tried very hard to talk her out of taking this step. None of us know what goes on behind closed doors and it became apparent that this marriage wasn't as happy as I had believed. The family I imagined to be perfect was falling apart and shattering like a broken mirror.

Cheryl was in no way prepared for divorce. She had put Johns' career ahead of her own. John paid the bills. Cheryl never had to worry about that. She had no significant income, no money saved, and no plans for the future. Even though I saw disaster looming, I could not dissuade her to at least delay her plans.

After we both calmed down, Cheryl told me that she had been unhappy for quite a while and tried to convince John to go for marriage counseling. He was content with the status quo and refused. When he finally agreed, the counselor advised that there was no point in trying to reconcile. The marriage was finished.

While married, Cheryl was a District Manager for Christmas Around the World, a business she ran out of her home. She earned several awards, including one for the "Most Congenial Attitude." The job offered great perks such as vacations at faraway places. My husband and I would stay with the children while Cheryl and John traveled.

For more than twenty years, I have worn the soft leather gloves they brought me from Florence, Italy. I recently noticed that one of the seams is opening. I will try to repair the seam with a couple of stitches so I can continue enjoying the gloves. A brilliantly colored stone bird from Brazil adorns my living room.

With three children of her own, Cheryl wanted to operate her own pre-school and daycare center from their home. John's lack of support in her endeavor was the proverbial straw that broke the camel's back that ended the marriage.

It made me happy that Cheryl didn't have to work outside her home while she had small children. Although most families at that time had two breadwinners, Cheryl had the luxury of staying home with her little ones. The children reflected the presence of a parent in the home. They were bright and well behaved. My daughter had no idea what divorce would mean and the negative effect it would have on the children. Aside from separating them from their father, there were huge financial problems ahead.

I saw history repeating itself. This was not what I had wanted for my daughter or grandchildren, but what I wanted didn't matter. I was tempted to say, "If you go through with this divorce without thinking it out, you cannot count on my help." But then Uncle Eugene's voice rang in my ear, telling me he would find the right charity to help me. I could not tell my child I would not help her. And help her I did until she was able to stand on her own two feet. I asked myself, if I, her mother, won't help her financially, who will? How will she care for her three young children?

Now I had two divorced children. All my grandchildren were growing up in single-parent homes.

That snowball picked up speed as it made its way down the hill.

CHAPTER VII
FLORIDA SINGLE MOM

In 1997, I made a fortieth birthday party for Cheryl in an Orlando restaurant. I looked at her friends sitting around the table. My daughter had outshone all others. None of the women at her party could compare. She was aware of her beauty and knew how to use it to her advantage. I must admit that she appeared happier single than married. All I wanted for her, and still want, is good health and happiness.

Without a profession, it is difficult to make a living in Florida. The state is full of retirees willing to work for minimum wages to supplement their Social Security checks. After many years of trying to find her niche in the job market, Cheryl finally found a position where she was happy and made a good living. The job came with good benefits, including the use of a company car. She was in outside sales and her outgoing personality made her an excellent sales person. Her clients were big institutions such as hospitals and nursing homes; her products were used to keep hospitals clean and sanitary. She received several awards for being a top-notch salesperson.

In 2004, while driving to see a client, Cheryl was rear-ended by a semi. She was seriously injured, and her car was demolished. It took several surgeries and a long period of recuperation to get her back on her feet. Eventually, she started her own company, Platinum Sales. Hospitals and institutions are still the focal point of her business.

Cheryl is a perfectionist. She has an impeccable work ethic; she always dresses and behaves in a professional manner. She raised three extremely capable, well-adjusted children. I have first-hand knowledge of the joys, as well as the trials and tribulations of raising three children as a single parent, and Cheryl deserves much credit for having done a great job. I hope she is as proud of her accomplishments as I am proud of her.

Cheryl's steady companion, Jim, is a welcome addition to my family.

Cheryl, my special baby daughter, I am very proud of you and I love you with all my heart.

SECTION THREE
HEARTACHES

CHAPTER I
AUNT BETSY'S FUNERAL

My dear Aunt Betsy passed away on December 8, 1994, and we buried her on the 11th. Her death stirred up a mountain of emotions within me. A great deal of unresolved pain surfaced. She looked beautiful at rest in her ivory lace dress. I had just talked to her a couple of days before. Although she complained of a cold, she had sounded pretty good. I had watched her slowly fade away during the past couple of years. When Henry and I had seen her that summer, we knew she was saying goodbye to us with a finality we didn't like. She told us that she had lived a long, good life; and since the quality of her life had diminished, she really did not care to go on.

Funerals always have been an emotional ordeal for me, probably because I was unable to lay my parents to rest and bring some closure to their lives. I relive their burial at every funeral I attend. My former boss Bob Brody had told me, as he lay dying of cancer, that it is easier to accept death as you grow older. I cannot agree. I have never really come to terms with the fact that we are born to die. Only the time we spend on earth and what we do with it varies.

Burying Aunt Betsy was more difficult than I could ever have imagined. Aside from the fact that I loved her dearly, she was the last link with my mother's generation. There were four sisters and their lives went in totally different directions. She undoubtedly had the best life of the four. They are all gone now and perhaps at last they are together again. It is difficult to handle the thought that my generation is the next one to go.

I truly appreciate Paul, his wife Jackie, and Tom's gift of their mother's sapphire ring. I wear it often, and while looking at the ring, I rub the sapphire, and imagine that -- as Dorothy clicked her heels to get back to Kansas – Aunt Betsy's presence is with me. While my eyes may mist, there is warmth in my heart. Now I have an angel sitting on each shoulder, my mother on one and Aunt Betsy on the other. Some might find this foolish, but nobody has ever come back to say otherwise. This thought comforts me.

The funeral opened many old wounds. I listened as Paul, Tom and Jeff, Paul's son, eulogized her, but when my cousin Peter was called upon to speak from notes he had obviously prepared, once again the old feeling of being left out grabbed me by the throat and choked me. When the Rabbi asked if anyone else would like to say something, I felt compelled to say my goodbye. I have no idea what I said. I only know my words came from the heart, and the rest didn't matter. I needed to tell her one more time how much I loved her and appreciated everything she had done for me. I had to bid her my final farewell, as I knew she was waiting to hear from me.

By the graveside, I reflected on my trip to Los Angeles several years earlier to celebrate Aunt Betsy and Uncle Eugene's golden anniversary. There had been no room for me at the family table. Aunt Betsy explained, "Peter helped pay for the party so he must sit with us." I had traveled two thousand miles to be there, but there was no room at their table for me? No room for one more chair? Once again, I asked myself how I fit into this family. As I pondered the past, I was brought back to the present when the Rabbi mentioned the names of all the grandchildren, including my cousin Peter's children. There was no mention of my own children. I felt the knife twist in my heart again. I wanted to shout, "I have children too!"

We bring children into the world and nurture them while they are totally dependent on us. Hopefully, under our guidance, they grow into independent, useful adults. That is our job as parents. When, however, children get past middle age, the roles reverse, and we, the parents, need our children emotionally more than they need us.

I think this is what happened in our case. During the last ten years or so of my aunt's life, while visiting in California, I was suddenly treated with unbelievable warmth and care. I asked myself, "Did this love and warmth exist all the time? Was I too blind to see it?" I don't think so. We all mellow with age. While we are young, everything is black and white; as we get older, the black and white slowly bleed into each other and blend into various shades of gray. As a parent myself, I now know that many choices must be made while raising a family.

Right or wrong, we have to live with our decisions when we have reached the point of no return.

I have truly enjoyed the relationship that slowly evolved between my Aunt Betsy and me over the last decade of her life. Whenever I visited, I felt comfortable and at home. When I was about fifty-five, she started to refer to me as her little girl. How ironic! I wish I could tell her one more time just how much she meant to me and how much I loved her. I lost her at a time when the bond was the strongest between us.

We never discussed my growing up years. That was behind us and there was no point to any further conversation. I also acquired an understanding from an adult viewpoint, which is very different from that of a child. My aunt did the best she could under very difficult circumstances. I came into her life while her wounds were still fresh from the loss of her sisters and parents. We both loved and were loved by the same people. There were no therapists to help us deal with our grief.

My unhappy teen years were neither my fault nor the Kuhn family's fault. The blame lies at the feet of Adolf Hitler and his diehard followers. They created "The Final Solution" of ridding Europe of all Jews. They robbed me of my happy home and tore my family apart. They stole my childhood. Of course, I was not the only one. They did the same thing to all Eastern European Jewish families.

CHAPTER II
UNCLE EUGENE

Uncle Eugene was totally lost by himself. He had bought and recently moved into a lovely apartment in an assisted living facility intended for two. He grieved deeply over the loss of Aunt Betsy, his lifelong companion. Throughout their younger years, he had been totally dependent on her for all his creature comforts. He had never known his way around a kitchen. Aunt Betsy always waited on him. During her last years, his life had been consumed with caring for her. On one of my visits, I watched him painstakingly set the table for breakfast. It must have taken him an hour to put out a couple of plates, cups and silverware. After her funeral, I never saw him again. Once I returned home, I called him weekly, but our conversations were always the same. He was very lonely and had the same complaints week after week. His memory was failing and he could no longer drive. Having been a CPA, keeping monetary records once had been second nature for him, but he was no longer able to handle his own finances. It hurt his pride to turn his financial matters over to someone else. In March 1996, as his 94th birthday approached I asked, "Would you like me to come and spend your birthday with you?" He was becoming senile and he was concerned that something inappropriate might occur if we were together alone. Of course, this was a figment of his imagination. I told him I would postpone my trip and would be with him for his ninety-fifth birthday, but he never reached that age. He fell in his apartment. By the time someone found him, he had bled excessively into the brain, fallen into a coma, and never recovered. He passed away on June 7, 1996, and we buried him on the 14th. I went to California for his funeral and stayed with Paul and Jackie.

Approximately ten years earlier, Paul's wife Jackie had been diagnosed with lymphoma. After being in remission for many years, her lymphoma recurred. Paul had lost his father and learned he had a sick wife at just about the same time. I wanted so much to help him, but I didn't know how. It must be twice as difficult for a physician to lose his loved ones and not be able to do anything about it. My heart truly went out to him.

Not many of us have the privilege to live to age ninety-four in a relatively healthy manner. It always amazed me that Paul's children for many years had two full sets of grandparents to love them and watch them grow. Most of us are not blessed with such fringe benefits.

I am grateful to Aunt Betsy and Uncle Eugene for caring enough to leave me an inheritance. However, I can't help wonder where they were when I was left alone with three young children. If they had offered some financial assistance at that time, it would have enabled me to go to a university and pursue a profession. The Jewish Federation was willing to pay my tuition, books and transportation, but I needed money for living expenses while in school. However, I managed. A year of business college gave me sufficient tools to raise my children without any outside help.

SECTION FOUR
GRANDCHILDREN ARE A BLESSING

CHAPTER I
COUNTING MY BLESSINGS

I have a very special relationship with all my grandchildren and try to spend some one-on-one time with each whenever possible. While I may love each child for a different reason, I love them all equally and unconditionally. It has been interesting and enjoyable to watch the various personalities emerge as they grew into adults.

All my grandchildren are musically gifted. They inherited their talent from their paternal great-grandfather, Theodore Kittay. Grandpa was an opera singer in his younger days and later a cantor at various synagogues.

Charles plays the guitar, writes music and sings. Jonathan played the sliding trombone and Adam the trumpet in their high school marching band. Ashley studied piano and plays quite well.

I grew up without my parents, my children grew up without their father and my grandchildren grew up in single-parent homes.

Most parents want better lives for their children than they had. I very much want a better life for my children, grandchildren and all future generations.

In spite of what I want, that snowball gets larger and larger as it rolls down the hill. Will that snowball melt before it rolls into my great-grandchildren's generation? I sure hope so.

CHAPTER II
CHARLES, MY FIRST GRANDCHILD

My first grandchild Charles, the son of Billy and Joyce, had a difficult childhood. While still an infant, his parents divorced. His mother married three times and had a son by each husband. Since he was my only grandchild in the Chicago area, he spent many weekends at my house. When it was time to go home, he usually left something behind. It was his way of making sure he could come back again. When Charles was about two-and-a-half, he told us, "We're moving to Coyoyado." I didn't want to believe it. When his stepfather, Dean, moved the family to Colorado, I cried my eyes out in fear that I might never see Charles again. Billy followed them; he wasn't going to be separated from his son. Joyce gave birth to Lester in Colorado. Charles now had a half brother. Charles with his mother, stepfather and infant brother, moved back to Chicago and settled in Streamwood. Once again, Billy followed them. It was good to have them back near me. When Billy and I went to pick up Charles, my toddler grandson flew into my son's arms yelling, "This is my real Daddy." He also told us about his baby brother, "Lechter." Joyce named her second child Lester after her father. This marriage also ended in divorce. Dean moved back to Colorado. He never looked after his son. Lester grew up without a father. In later years, Charles took Lester under his wings and tried to be a father figure to him.

Joyce's third husband, Bobby, was a drunken abusive hillbilly. Joyce was pregnant again, this time with Bobby, Jr. While Charles made some vague references to his unhappy home life, he was not specific. However, his complaints were sufficient to arouse Billy's suspicions that something was wrong in his son's home. Once Billy realized that Charles was in an abusive home, he contacted an attorney to fight for his child's custody. I tried my best to mother and nurture my grandchild. The attorney advised that the only way to obtain custody of his son was to prove Joyce an unfit mother. This was a very tall, expensive order. Fate assisted Billy in his custody fight. Inadvertently, he learned that Charles's teachers were aware of his abusive home situation and contacted the Department of Children and Family Services. A DCFS investigation proved Joyce to be an unfit mother. All three of her children were removed from her home. Charles was about twelve years old at that time. He was lucky that his father was eager to take him and raise him. The other two children from Joyce's subsequent marriages were placed in foster homes.

My son was a very loving, caring father. He tightened the reins on Charles, set some rules for acceptable and unacceptable behavior and taught him right from wrong. Billy spent all his free time with his son and devoted his life to raising him. While attending Niles North High School in Skokie, my grandson made the honor role. We were so proud of him. After graduation, he attended local neighborhood colleges, but he really wasn't interested in school. His true ambition was to become a musician or a movie star.

Charles was close to my husband Henry and his son Mike. Henry was a very good Grandpa to all the grandchildren. Since Charles was the only little one in our area, he spent a great deal of time with us. Henry often made breakfast for him and played with him. Charles learned his colors by playing with a stack of poker chips on our dining room floor.

In 2001, when Henry was very ill, Charles came to the hospital and told us, "I enlisted in the Army." Although I had some reservations, Henry encouraged him. It was peacetime and we thought military service would be good for him. Aside from discipline, we thought the army would provide him with vocational training. He received his basic training in South Carolina. His father, his Uncle Steve and I attended his graduation, the completion of his basic training. We took his brother Lester and a friend along. From there, he was transferred to an army base in the California desert.

Charles came home on leave to attend the funeral of his maternal grandmother. When he had difficulty breathing during the night, his dad took him to the hospital. He was immediately admitted. Various specialists were called in to diagnose his illness. After what appeared to be an eternity, an infectious disease doctor determined he had Coccidioidomycosis, commonly known as Valley Fever, a very serious illness caused by spores in the desert. Doctors in the Midwest are not familiar with this condition. It was necessary to surgically clear his lungs and he was on a ventilator for a week. Charles was a very sick young man. Thanks to excellent medical care, he recovered and later returned to his army unit. Eventually, he received a medical discharge.

His discharge came at a perfect time. The U.S. had just gone to war with Iraq for the second time, and every available soldier was shipped out to the Middle East. Charles received monthly disability benefits and college tuition from the army. Once again, he enrolled in college. This time he completed and received a two-year certificate from Oakton College and later a Bachelor's Degree In Philosophy from Northeastern University. We tried to tell him he would have difficulty finding a job in his chosen field, but he was stubborn and wouldn't listen to anyone. We were proud of him when he received his degree, but he did have trouble finding a job.

While working at the Hilton Hotel as a bellman, he met Angela, an attractive young woman who was in the navy, stationed at Great Lakes. After a whirlwind courtship, Angela and Charles married and moved to the West Coast where Angela was stationed. Charles is currently a car salesman. He recently started graduate school seeking a career in human resources. However, his ambition to succeed in show business still lingers. Charles and Angela have blessed me with my first great grandchild, Caden Alexander, born November 10, 2008. Caden and I have not yet met. I look forward to holding him in my arms soon. In the meantime, I admire and talk to his pictures posted on my refrigerator. I hope Angela and Charles are happy so that Caden can have a stable, happy home.

Charles, my darling, I love you and I am very proud of you.

CHAPTER III
MY FLORIDA GRANDCHILDREN

My three Florida grandchildren were born to Cheryl and John. While their lives were not quite as traumatic as Charles's, they too grew up in a single-parent home.

A. JONATHAN

Jonathan, the eldest, was born in Bartlett, Illinois on April 26, 1982. From the moment he came into this world, he looked like his father. Jonathan and I truly enjoyed each other. While he was still an only child, on a Christmas morning, he opened a gift and said, "Oh my God!" I couldn't believe those words came out of the mouth of this little tot. When he got a bit older, I bought him a battery operated sit-in Jeep. Whenever I said, "Jonathan, where are you going?"

He always answered, "Chicago."

Jonathan played Little League baseball. He had a strong arm. While at bat, his team chanted, "Let's go Jonathan, let's go."

When Jonathan's baby brother Adam was about two years old, Cheryl told her children, "We are going to have another baby." Jonathan thought for a moment and then blurted out, "Does that mean we are going to send Adam back?" One sibling was sufficient competition for him.

Jonathan, always a very conscientious student, did well in school. From the time he was in the sixth grade, he knew he wanted to be a pharmacist.

During one of my visits, he approached me and asked, "Grandma, we are studying the Holocaust at school. Could you come and speak to my class?"

I was stunned. Nobody ever asked me to talk about the Holocaust. I had worked so hard to push it out of my mind. At that moment all I could say was, "Jonathan, I have to sleep on this. I will give you my answer tomorrow." I spent a sleepless night, tossing and turning, thinking whether I would be able to talk to a classroom of eighth graders. I decided to give it a try. That was the beginning of my involvement with Holocaust related issues. My talk was well received. When Adam and Ashley reached the eighth grade, I was invited again to share my story with their classmates.

After high school, Jonathan attended Florida State University where he received his Bachelor's Degree in Science. For his graduate studies, he is at Hampton University in Virginia. He is currently finishing his internship in pharmacy and will receive his Ph.D. in May 2010. I hope to be there to applaud him. Jonathan is also an accomplished poker player and loves Las Vegas. He has accepted a job offer with CVS in the Las Vegas area. Fitness is very important to him. Like his mother, he spends considerable time in the gym.

Jonathan, my darling, I love you and I am very proud of you.

B. ADAM

Adam, my Florida middle grandchild, was born on April 4, 1984. He always admired and looked up to his big brother. Jonathan gave him rides in the jeep I had bought him. Their imaginary trips took them either to Chicago or Sanibel Island, where the family had vacationed.

School came easily for Adam. He and his older brother have quite different personalities. Adam is a quiet brooder. As a youngster, he always knew what he wanted and often disagreed with his parents. Through the years, we have often repeated some of his cute sayings. On one of our visits, Adam met us at the airport and immediately took to my husband. He really didn't know Henry, but as soon as Adam saw him, he said, "I go with Grandpa."

He became Grandpa's sidekick. He set up plastic bowling pins in the garage so he could bowl with Grandpa. When they got older, both Florida boys became active in bowling leagues.

When Adam was about three, he came to the motel where my husband and I stayed to play in the wading pool. When he had to go to the bathroom, he got out of the pool and said, "I gotta pee; I go by myself; I know how; room 115." We handed him the card key. In a few minutes he was back with a long face saying, "I can't open the doo'." I took him by the hand and together we opened that door. Adam often sang himself to sleep in the car. "Zip-A-Dee-Doo-Dah" was one of his favorites. At his preschool graduation, he received a rousing ovation for his rendition of "I'm taking home a baby bumble bee."

Like his brother, Adam also attended FSU. He graduated with a degree in Electrical Engineering. During his senior year, he received a job offer from Siemens Engineering, starting immediately upon receipt of his degree. Since then, he has traveled all over this country and abroad on behalf of his employer. He never knows where his next assignment will take him.

Adam is the family's computer expert. We all call him for advice.

Adam loves his girl Kate and his job. They are a great couple. Kate, a pretty blond, is a registered nurse. They recently moved into their newly built home. I hope to see it soon. While in Rome on a cruise, Adam presented Kate with an engagement ring. Adam left on a cruise with his girlfriend and returned with his fiancée. They are a handsome, loving couple. The wedding is planned for March 2011. I sure hope to be there.

Adam, my darling, I am very proud of you and I love you very much. I wish you and Kate a wonderful life.

C. ASHLEY, MY PETUNIA

Ashley, my baby's baby, was born December 16, 1987. I nicknamed her my little Petunia at a very early age, and it has stuck with her. She was and remains my precious one and only granddaughter. She was Mama's girl and sat on her Mama's hip while Cheryl washed dishes or cleaned house. Ashley was a slow talker. The doctor said that if her two brothers wouldn't hand her everything she wanted, she would talk. Once she started talking, she never stopped. My daughter dressed her in pretty matching outfits. She looked like a little porcelain doll. I always liked sailor style dresses on little girls. At the end of summer, I shopped for end-of-season bargains for my Florida grandchildren. There, they could wear summer clothes all year. I had a great time picking out t-shirts, shorts and sundresses, wrapped them with love and tissue paper and sent them to Orlando.

On one of my visits, I got weepy at the thought of going home, leaving my family behind. Ashley said, "Grandma, don't cry. We cry when we get to the airport."

As she got older, she, too, played Little League ball. She was quite a sight as she stood at home plate waiting for the pitch with bat on her shoulder, helmet on her head, shaking her little butt.

Ashley was enrolled in ballet school when she was about three. She really didn't like it. While my husband and I were babysitting, we took her to her ballet class. Grandpa tried to bribe her and told her, "Ashley, after ballet we'll go to McDonalds for chicken nuggets."

Ashley answered, "No, we have to go to the mall."

"Why," asked my husband?

"Cause at the mall we get free ice cream."

We often took the three little ones to "Show Biz," now known as Chuck E Cheese, where we bought tokens for them to play various games. Ashley couldn't talk yet, but she knew how to stretch out her arm and hold out her little palm for more tokens.

Like her brothers, Ashley did well in school. After high school, she attended the University of Florida in Gainesville. I watched with pride when she received her Bachelor of Science degree in the spring of 2009. She is now on a cross-country bike trip, from New Hampshire to Vancouver. The trip is sponsored by Bike and Build, an organization that raises money and helps build homes for the needy. Even though Ashley is the only girl among my grandchildren, she seems to be the most adventurous one. She wants to see and experience all she can.

My little petunia has blossomed into a very accomplished and attractive young woman. She plans on attending graduate school and pursuing a career in public health.

Ashley, my little petunia, I love you and I am very proud of you.

SECTION FIVE
HENRY

CHAPTER I
ENTER HENRY

Steve was no longer living at home, Billy was married and had a child, and Cheryl had graduated college and was engaged. For the first time, I was about to have an empty nest.

In January 1980, while working at the estate planning law firm, a long-time acquaintance called and told me about a recently divorced gentleman who was looking for a lady friend. She asked if she could give him my phone number. Since I had nothing to lose, I consented. Soon, I received a call from a man who identified himself as Henry Schwartz. He seemed pleasant and during our brief conversation, he asked if I would like to have a cup of coffee with him. That phone call, once again, took my life in a different direction.

Henry rang the bell to pick me up. The first thing out of his mouth was, "My, you're a pretty lady." He was a good-looking man, impeccably dressed, with a warm smile. The coffee date led to a dinner date, and many more dinners followed. We slowly got acquainted and learned about each other's lives. He seemed to be kind and considerate, a gentleman in every respect.

Henry had a sterling employment record. He had spent a lifetime working for Goldblatt's as a furniture buyer. His steady employment record impressed me. In April 1980, he was preparing to go to North Carolina to the annual furniture market. When he never called to say, "So long, I'll see you soon," I was miffed and decided that if that's the way he wanted it, it was "So long Henry," as far as I was concerned.

As I walked around in a snit, our mutual friend called and told me that Henry had had a heart attack and was in Northwestern Hospital. While I was sorry he was sick, it gave him a legitimate excuse for not calling. The hospital informed me that although he was doing well, he was in ICU and couldn't talk on the phone. Once he was out of ICU, I jumped in a cab on my lunch hour and went to visit him. To my surprise, he was the healthiest looking heart attack patient I had ever seen. He had been sunning himself on the roof and acquired a very becoming tan.

After his discharge, Henry recuperated at his sister Eva's home. She invited me to dinner, and the two of us instantly clicked. She not only made me very comfortable, but within a half hour, it felt as if we had been lifelong friends. Eva and her husband Ben lived downtown in an elegant high-rise condo on Lake Shore Drive. They had turned two units into one to create a large, impressive apartment. A uniformed doorman assisted people coming and going. Glass elevators carried their passengers to and from their apartments. I soon became a regular at their dinner table. From their balcony overlooking Lake Michigan, we watched the yachts, decorated in vibrant colors, float by during the annual Venetian Night Festival.

A few weeks later, Henry was ready to go home and eventually returned to work. We continued seeing each other more and more frequently. As our pasts unfolded, I felt we were on common ground as he, too, had dealt with a mentally ill former mate. The difference was that I felt guilty for having left Danny, while he felt guilty for having stayed with his wife Rose for so many years while their son's mental problems escalated. He blamed Rose for all his son's problems. We each had a troubled son who needed to get on track. After many discussions about our past and current problems, we began to talk about marriage. While he did not look it, Henry was eighteen years older than I was, a considerable age difference. Our goal was to make each other happy and help guide our troubled children toward becoming self-sufficient adults.

Henry told me about Mike's serious emotional problems. Getting Mike well was his priority. Henry attributed his son's problems to his ex-wife, Mike's mother. Mike was unable to get along with his teachers and his peers in high school and dropped out. He was diagnosed with Obsessive Compulsive Disorder (OCD) and schizophrenia. During his teens, Mike had been under psychiatric care, in and out of hospitals. When Mike reached his twenties, his mother, Rose, wanted to institutionalize him but Henry was determined to care for his son at home. While there were many areas of contention between Rose and Henry, the main reason for divorce was their opposing approach to Mike's care. Mike was intelligent and able to discuss current events and various sports. His emotional problems had no bearing on his IQ. His inner voices and thoughts were his demons.

Henry took me home to meet his son Mike. When he opened the door, I saw an elegantly furnished, spotlessly clean apartment. The white velvet sofa, the heavy gold drapery with sheer white curtains, the porcelain lamps, the oil paintings in the living room and the mural in the master bedroom took me by surprise. We walked into a dining room that begged for company. I never had been able to afford this type of living. I always loved to entertain, but never had the space to set an attractive table in a lovely dining room. Little did I suspect that this home would become an ivory tower where no one was permitted entry.

Henry had two children, Anita and Mike. Anita had a handsome seven-year-old son, Tony. She was a very ambitious and accomplished young woman. She divorced soon after her son's birth and moved back home until she finished college, attended graduate school, became an accountant and later a CPA. Tony was a warm, handsome child with large dark eyes and lots of dark curly hair. He liked my cooking and told me, "Grandma, your ribs taste better than Carson's," a local restaurant specializing in barbequed ribs. He immediately stole my heart. Anita was polite but a bit reticent. She had not yet recovered from her parents' divorce and I sensed a bit of estrangement between her and her father. I never met Rose, Henry's first wife.

At first it appeared that Mike liked me and I was happy to try and contribute to his recovery. I was so touched that I had tears in my eyes when Mike asked if he could call me Mother. After all, his mother was still alive but the two didn't communicate.

Henry's son Mike and my son Billy were both in their early twenties. As our children got acquainted, our troubled sons started to socialize. Billy took Mike to meet his friends and got him out of the house and among people. Mike was crazy about my toddler grandson, Charles. We thought the association between our sons might be beneficial to both.

After dating for approximately a year, Henry and I were married by Judge Sullivan at the Skokie Court House in the presence of our families. We celebrated our marriage with a luncheon at the Hyatt House in Lincolnwood. Then we headed to Florida and spent our honeymoon with Eva, Henry's sister, and her husband Ben. Eva, unfortunately, had terminal cancer. She wanted us to spend some time with her and we were eager to please her.

The first inkling of trouble on the home front came while we were in Florida. Mike called hysterically, complaining about my son Billy. Evidently the two boys got into an argument. When Henry and I got home, the house was a disaster. Mike had smashed whatever came his way. He blamed my son for insulting him and causing his rage. He wanted to tell me his side of the story. I knew I couldn't get caught in the middle. I told Mike that both he and Billy were grown men and I didn't want to hear either side. This was between them and had nothing to do with me. However, this changed the relationship between Mike and me. He started resenting me. Like a young child, Mike was jealous of the time his father spent with me.

We had a volatile situation on our hands and urgently needed help with defusing it. Although Henry told me that Mike had been destructive in the past, I'd never seen him behave that way. It scared me. We started seeing a therapist. It didn't take me very long to figure out what really was wrong in this household.

As I listened to Henry give some background information, I realized that in Henry's eyes, the entire world had hurt his son. His mother hurt him, the teachers hurt him, and all the kids in school hurt him. Everyone was wrong except Mike. It was, "Poor Mike, we must do whatever he says; otherwise he is going to destroy our home."

I said to myself, hold it! Who is in charge in this house, Mike or his father? Henry was scared of his son; he was unable to make any decisions without Mike's permission. He did not hesitate to tell me that my son's presence upset Mike.

Too bad, I thought, now you are talking about my child. At this point, I was ready to leave Henry, but I had made the mistake of moving into his apartment, and I had given away all my furnishings and belongings. The contemplation of having to start all over again petrified me. What had happened to the man who had said he welcomed my children and didn't want to interfere with the relationship between my children and me? My sweet Henry had turned into Papa Bear protecting his cub.

Through the years, out of necessity, I had become a very independent woman who had lived without a husband for fifteen years. I told Henry I was not accustomed to asking permission to buy whatever I wanted, and he said that was fine with him. We also discussed our plans for the future. I would work for about five years and then retire.

I loved my husband. He was a very decent, honest man, but when it came to his son, he was an outright liar. He didn't mean to lie; he was just a good salesman who was able to justify everything in his son's favor. He was truly killing his son with love. One therapist pointed out that Henry needed "a poor sick boy" and in fact Mike was being a good boy by obliging. We were also told that if Mike were a minor, the Department of Children and Family Services would consider Henry's behavior abusive and would remove Mike from our home.

One of the most revealing statements that came from Mike during a therapy session was, "My dad has no credibility." And therein lies the basis of Mike's problems. The child was leading the father instead of the father leading the child. Like a typical two-year-old, Mike knew that if he threw a tantrum, his father would give in and allow him to do as he wished. I spent many sleepless nights trying to find a way to rescue Mike from his father's clutches, but it became obvious that they satisfied certain needs for each other. There was nothing I could do. I was the outsider in this triangle. Once again, I was on the outside looking in.

CHAPTER II
BILLY GROWS UP

Observing Henry's relationship with his son made me take a second look at the way I was raising my son, Billy. I saw Henry smothering Mike. If nothing else good came from that, I decided that I could not and would not do this to my son! With the aid of an insightful therapist, I started to withdraw financial aid from Billy. He called me one evening and asked me to meet him. He was at rock bottom. He admitted he had a problem. We sat over a cup of coffee and talked for a long time. I reminded him that he had a young son who needed him and told him he needed professional help. He agreed and took my advice. He had just taken his first step toward recovery.

Pulling the rug out from under him was the most difficult thing I ever did as a mother. It pained me to watch him struggle. I was committed to follow the therapist's advice and let Billy solve his own problems. It was a slow process, but it worked. For me, it would have been much easier to reach out and help than to watch him struggle. However, I learned that my help impeded his progress. I could see his self-confidence and self-esteem grow as he accomplished more and more on his own and became independent. One thing was for sure. Billy loved his little boy dearly, and Charles was probably the catalyst for getting his dad to turn his life around and accept responsibility. Billy took his life into his own hands and did whatever was necessary to earn a living, create a career and above all, raise his son. He made me very proud.

CHAPTER III
LIFE WITH HENRY

For years I had thoroughly psychoanalyzed every man I met and even considered dating. I didn't want to repeat my past mistake of marrying a sick man. Unfortunately, I misjudged this situation.

Henry and I went through several therapists. As soon as they suggested treating Mike differently, Henry decided the therapists were no good and he would not go back. One excellent therapist stated that usually it is the parent and the therapist who together bring a child into line. In this case, it was the parent and the child who formed an alliance against the therapist.

While Henry dropped out, I continued with therapy for my own sanity. Frankly, every therapist I saw felt I should get out of this marriage, but they were much younger than I was. I just could not entertain the possibility of spending the little money I had on starting all over again. So somewhere down the line, I made the decision that I would stick it out. I've had moments when I felt that I sold my life for a bowl of porridge. However, it is also true that this marriage replaced my loneliness with companionship, improved my standard of living and enabled me to do things for my children and grandchildren that I could not have done otherwise. Our relationship was a two-way street. We were both better off together than apart. My salary and the rental income from my condo enriched both our lives. Despite our problems, I loved him and he loved me.

In all other respects, Henry was a very good husband. An early riser, he made breakfast for me and brought it to our bedroom so I could have something to eat while I dressed for work. In the afternoon, he got home before I did. By the time I walked in the door, dinner was on the table waiting for me. He washed the dishes before I finished my meal. He shopped for groceries and did the laundry.

Henry always remembered me on special occasions. He had excellent taste and he bought me lovely gifts. They knew him well at the neighborhood ladies wear shop. Both my husband and the saleslady Stella knew the type of clothes I liked and the styles that flattered my figure. Together they built me a great wardrobe. I often received compliments on the suits I wore to the office. At an office Christmas party, my boss Bill looked at me and said, "Agnes I pay you too well. That's a beautiful outfit."

I said, "My paycheck didn't buy this, it was a gift from my husband."

We took some great vacations. Cruising was my favorite. For my sixtieth birthday, Henry took me on an unforgettable trip to Hawaii. We flew to Oahu and cruised the islands. His daughter Anita upgraded our coach flight to first class with her mileage. It was a luxurious, great trip. The flight attendants hovered over us, offering food and drinks.

We spent some weekends at the Marriott in Lincolnshire. There, we watched a play, enjoyed some fine dining and relaxed at the pool. Our other favorite get-away spot was Nippersink, a resort about an hour's drive from home. It offered a package of lodging, good food, sports and entertainment. We needed to make time for just the two of us. Away from home, we were quite compatible and happy.

Life is full of compromises and I had made mine. Undoubtedly, once again I had found a mate with some mental problems. While Henry's problems were nothing like Danny's, my second husband had a sick relationship with his son. There was nothing I could do about it. Henry did not like confrontations. He never wanted to discuss our differences. While I needed to talk, he wanted to sweep all our problems under the rug. After a while, the rug began to bulge. Occasionally my Hungarian temper got the best of me. I exploded. However, once my anger surfaced, I was able to put it behind me.

I left him twice during our twenty-year marriage, but I returned each time. Cheryl, John, Jonathan and Adam came from Florida to commemorate Adam's first birthday with us. We invited family and friends to join in the celebration at our condo association's party room. Henry was upset by the fuss and commotion and was unbelievably rude to my children and our guests. As soon as Cheryl and family returned to Florida, I packed my bag and left to stay with friends. After several days, Henry apologized profusely and admitted he was wrong. I made it clear that if he ever pushed me again to the point where I needed to leave, I would not return. Bouncing in and out of the house was not my idea of a marriage.

I left again just before my sixty-fifth birthday. I had recently retired. Henry's health was declining and I had planned to make an office for myself out of the den. I was doing a little work from home and wanted my own space. The money I earned went into a joint account. I ran into very strong opposition from Henry. Mike was used to watching television in that room. Once again, he did not want to upset his son. It was all right to upset me, but not Mike, his poor sick boy, who by now was in his forties and had never worked a day in his life. Henry refused to see that allowing Mike to do nothing day after day was not a solution for his son's mental problems. I couldn't understand why Mike couldn't have watched television in his own room.

I needed some breathing space and time to think. I went to stay with my son Steve. Henry had a rough time with this decision. He knew I was right, but he was unable to say "no" to Mike. By this time, we had been married about eighteen years and Henry's health was failing. While he would not change his mind about the den, he pleaded with me to come home. I knew he was sick and needed me. I swallowed my pride and returned.

Diabetes is an insidious disease. It quietly lurks in the body while it slowly destroys vital organs. Henry was very good about watching his diet. His blood sugar was always under control. Diabetes, heart disease and kidney failure often go together. When Henry was seventy-five, he had triple bypass surgery. While he was in intensive care, I learned about "Sundown Syndrome," a situation where an elderly patient hallucinates after dark. The doctors had trouble finding the reason for his slow recovery. His fever spiked. After many tests, they determined he had an infected gall bladder. He received antibiotics and I was able to bring him home. We knew he needed gall bladder surgery, but we were trying to buy time to give him a chance to recover from the open-heart operation. Henry wasn't home very long when I rushed him to Weiss Memorial Hospital where his gangrenous gall bladder was removed. The surgeon told me if we had waited another day, it would have burst and the gangrene would have spread throughout his abdomen. They did an old-fashioned abdominal cut because they felt that laparoscopic surgery would keep him under anesthesia too long. One serious surgery on top of another was hard on Henry's system. Once again, he had a slow recovery. Then he developed a bleeding ulcer that had to be healed.

In August 1999, his kidneys failed and it became inevitable that in order to survive, he needed dialysis three times a week. He didn't want it. The doctor convinced him to at least try it. He could always quit, but in order to stay alive, he had to have dialysis. Henry reluctantly agreed, but he hated it. He was totally depleted after each session. All he could do was come home and sleep. The first couple of months, I stayed with him during each dialysis session. Later, I found transportation for him through the Jewish Council for the Elderly. That made my life a bit easier. During the last couple years of his life, I called 911 several times when he went into congestive heart failure and the paramedics rushed him by ambulance to the hospital. Because the symptoms were so similar, I couldn't tell for sure whether he was having a heart attack or his blood sugar was dangerously low. He became totally dependent on me and even gave up driving when he turned eighty-five.

Beginning in January 2001, Henry spent more time in the hospital than at home. He would barely be discharged when we had to readmit him. I sat by his side day after day. Sometimes, during the night the nurses would call and ask me to come to the hospital to calm him down. He would hallucinate and become frightened. Because of his weak heart, they were unable to sedate him.

In February, we were watching television in Henry's hospital room when a commercial caught his eye. They were selling red silk roses for Valentine's Day. He knew he would be unable to shop for me. He said, "Honey, please order a dozen roses, no two dozen, put them on your credit card, and I will pay you back. Be sure you remind me to repay you."

The roses are still blooming in my living room. They bring back loving, fond memories. That was the last gift Henry was able to give me.

After a long hospital stay, the doctor felt he should go to a nursing home for rehab to regain some strength and steady his walk. When we arrived, he looked around and said, "You brought me to an old people's home, I want to go home."

It broke my heart. I said, "Come on honey, let's go home." The administrator of the facility did her best to convince him to stay, but he would not change his mind. Soon he was readmitted to the hospital.

The dialysis machine was sucking away Henry's life. Once again, the doctors wanted to send him to the nursing home for rehab. The only way he would agree was if I stayed with him. He was only there for a couple of days when he said, "I feel sick," and I watched his eyes roll back. If I hadn't been there, nobody would have noticed his distress. Upon my insistence, they called an ambulance that took him back to the hospital. He had suffered another heart attack.

No matter how hard I tried to keep him alive, Henry was slipping away. He had a problem holding down food. Our family doctor said that regardless of what was done for him, he was a very sick man and had only a short time to live. He lost control of his bowels and they started diapering him. His heartbeat became erratic. An angiogram revealed severe blockages, and the cardiologist informed us that if we did nothing, he would die within a couple of days. If they attempted angioplasty, it would be very high risk and he could die on the table.

I was confronted with a monumental decision. How could I deprive him of possibly living a little longer? The family urged me to agree to the procedure. The angioplasty went well and stents were inserted into three arteries. However, while the surgery improved Henry's circulation, it did not fix his damaged heart. His arrhythmia became more and more difficult to control. His heart was not strong enough to allow him to get out of bed.

At this point, our doctor decided that he would be better off at a rehab facility where he could receive physical therapy as well as dialysis. Very few rehabs offer dialysis.

During a blizzard, Henry was transferred by ambulance to Swedish Covenant Hospital's rehab unit. He had stopped eating. His only nourishment came from Glucerna, a food supplement for diabetics, he drank through a straw. The nursing staff at Swedish Covenant Hospital found a large bedsore on his back and sores on his heels. A wound care specialist was called in and began treating his sores aggressively. The ravages of diabetes and his inability to eat meant the sores would not heal. In the meantime, he still received dialysis three times a week. The wound care doctor informed us that the sore on his back was getting worse each day. The only way it could get better was if Henry had "flap over" surgery. The doctor explained that this was major surgery where they take a muscle and flap it over the open wound in order to allow it to heal.

Henry was much too weak to undergo another major surgery. His brother, niece, and I talked to the internist who recommended that we put Henry on hospice and let him go. He had no chance of getting well.

The following morning, I got a call from the hospital telling me that Henry had taken a turn for the worse. By the time I got there, he was gone. After all the hours I had spent at his bedside, he died alone. I felt terrible that I wasn't with him and was unable to hold him when he took his last breath on March 29, 2001. In accordance with Henry's wishes, he was cremated. Later, he was eulogized at a memorial service. The temple was filled with family and friends. Everybody from my office attended the services. It comforted me to know so many cared.

CHAPTER IV
DESERTED AGAIN

I had been very close to Henry's family from the time I first met them. A warm, close-knit family, they welcomed me with open arms. They filled my emotional needs. I was eager to fit in. I trusted them and considered them to be my family. The immediate family consisted of Henry's daughter Anita, his son Mike, his sister Lillian, his brother Ray and Ray's wife, Faye. When Henry and I met, Anita was divorced and had a handsome young son, Tony. He was about seven, playing T-ball. Later, Anita moved to the West Coast where she met and married Steve Hill. Together they gave us another grandchild, Brian. Tony was about 18 when Brian was born.

There were many nephews and nieces. Henry often told me that his family would always be there for me, even after he was gone. Before we married and throughout our marriage, Henry always assured me that his brother would take care of Mike financially while his sister Lillian would take care of him physically. I had no reason to doubt him. Both Ray and Faye assured me many times during Henry's long illness that they would be there to help get Mike out of the house. Ray even said that should it become necessary, he would bodily remove Mike from the apartment after Henry's death.

Unfortunately, Ray acquired a selective memory and could not recall his promise to me. Henry had discussed with Ray that he was leaving his apartment to me. As a matter of fact, Henry told me Ray tried to talk him out of it. Shortly after we married, we drew up reciprocal wills. We knew that whenever one of us died, the surviving partner would need both properties to live in relative comfort. Therefore, we made each other the principal beneficiary in our wills. Had I predeceased Henry, he would have inherited my apartment. To compensate for leaving my apartment to Henry, I bought life insurance and named my children as beneficiaries.

After Henry's will was read and it became obvious that my husband left me everything while I was alive and nothing to his son, my relationship with his family totally collapsed. Ray said, "My brother would never sign a will like this; there is no signature." Without actually saying it, he called me a crook.

I told him, "Only the original will has a signature. The original has been filed with the court. Ask Mark, your son, an attorney, to pick up a copy from the courthouse."

His sister Lillian said, "We are Mike's advocates."

I wondered why Mike needed an advocate to protect him from me. Couldn't the family see they were contributing to the ever-growing chasm between Mike and me? I became the wicked witch. The family's action reinforced Mike's thinking that I was his enemy.

The Schwartz family's behavior toward me broke my heart. The twenty plus years of warm relationship were now over. I never had any reason before to doubt their loyalty. Blood became thicker than water and they felt that they could not talk to both Mike and to me. I still can't understand why.

I certainly never wanted anything but the best for Mike. I don't know why Henry thought his family would look after his son. It could have been because Ray had always been there to help. Sometimes Ray came in the middle of the night to calm Mike when he became too boisterous for Henry to handle. I would have been willing to do anything to help Mike, but I could not live under the same roof with him. After Henry's demise, Mike and I lived together without speaking to each other for a year. Mike never liked to bathe or wear clean clothes. His father had to prod him to shower and wash his clothes. With his father gone, he never bathed. The apartment reeked of body odor. The neighbors complained of the stench in the hallway. It was an impossible situation.

Henry had played a dirty trick. He had told each of us in private what we wanted to hear. According to Mike, his Dad told him that after his death he could live in the condo for the rest of his life. This became Mike's mantra as he repeated it over and over to the attorneys and the judge. Henry had told Ray that he left a non-existent $50,000 to Mike, while he told me that Ray would make sure I had no problem with Mike or any responsibility for him.

Henry did not like confrontation, and by telling each of us what we wanted to hear, he avoided a possible altercation. Ray accused me of having the will drawn up by someone I knew and slipping in language without Henry's knowledge. Henry was a very bright businessman, and the will he signed was drafted exactly to his specifications. He understood the conditions of the will thoroughly. It is common sense that if Henry had left Mike $50,000, Mike's name would have been on a bank account or documented in Henry's will. I can only surmise that it was easier for Henry to tell Ray that he left Mike $50,000 than to tell the truth.

The Schwartz family was there for me while they needed me. Once I was totally spent emotionally, they had no further use for me. They found it easier to put the blame on me than on their diseased brother.

After nursing Henry through his prolonged illness and coming home to Mike every night, I was totally exhausted. Mike never asked about his father or how the day went. When Henry's death became imminent, I said, "Mike, your father is dying. If you want to see him alive, now is the time to go see him." Mike didn't budge. Probably Mike's illness prevented him from saying goodbye to his dad. He wrote a eulogy that his Uncle Ray presented at the memorial service, but Mike didn't attend.

Henry was sixty-five when we married. His previous divorce had taken most of his savings. He owned a lovely condo with a mortgage, but he had very little money. He was nearing the end of his career when he lost his job with his long-time employer. He had received some severance pay after Goldblatt's permanently closed their furniture department. Following that, for several years Henry worked for his brother Ray as a manufacturer's representative.

It is puzzling that while Henry was totally absorbed in caring for Mike, he made no plans for Mike's future. He had a small life insurance policy from the army, which he cashed in. I suggested that he keep the policy and make Mike the beneficiary. He didn't want to do that. Many years later, we opened a certificate of deposit and I suggested that he name Mike as the secondary beneficiary rather than his estate. He didn't want that either. I can only wonder whether Henry was venting his anger towards Mike or towards Ray. I know Henry was disappointed when Ray made it clear that should Henry die, he would not take Mike into his home.

I had worked during our marriage and did not quit until Henry's health deteriorated to the point where I felt he needed me at home with him. Undoubtedly, going to work would have been easier than staying at home watching my husband suffer. Henry was not a rich man when we married and I certainly did not marry him for his money. Actually, I had more money than he had at that time. During our marriage, I had an opportunity to save for my "golden years." Most of our savings came from the rental of my apartment on Christiana. Everything went into joint accounts. Had I died first, his family would not have complained if he inherited everything.

Not once has anyone in his family called to see how I was doing or ask whether I was still alive. Since Mike made it clear that he was not going to move, I was forced to take legal action to evict him. This turned the family even more against me. They did not understand that Mike was not going to move unless he was forced to do so. I had given him many extensions, but on the advice of my attorney, I finally agreed to turn the eviction papers over to the sheriff. I would have much rather given Mike the money than spend it on attorney's fees.

I don't know how Eva and Ben's daughter Sharon got into the picture, but Sharon became friendly with Mike and earned his trust. At the last minute, Mike accepted the fact that he must move. She helped him find an apartment and was there with him on the first day of March 2002 when Mike actually moved out. He took nothing except the piano and his television. I had no problem with that. I tried to wish him well when he left and told him that if he ever needed anything, I'd be there for him. He refused my handshake and did not want to hear what I had to say. I hoped that the push out the door, the "tough love," would force him to seek badly needed medical attention. Had I allowed him to stay with me, he would have continued to vegetate on the floor watching TV for the rest of his life. With the many new anti-psychotic drugs on the market, I hoped he would make a life for himself. The last time I talked to Ray, he accused me of buying furniture with Mike's money. The Schwartz family needed a scapegoat, and I became "it."

I've asked myself many times, "What have I done to be deserted by loved ones over and over again?" I don't know, but for the fourth time in my life, once again, I had been abandoned.

CHAPTER V
THE CIRCLE CLOSES

It was close to midnight on Thursday, January 12, 2006 when my telephone rang. As a rule, nobody calls me after 10:00 P.M. Anita's husband Steve was on the other end of the line. I knew his parents had been ill; they were up in years. Anita and Steve had visited them in Detroit right after Christmas. I presumed he was calling to tell me that something happened to his mom, who had suffered multiple strokes before their visit. Little by little it came out that Myra, Ray's daughter, called Anita to tell her that Mike had died Wednesday and was being buried on Friday. Bad enough that nobody had let me know of Mike's demise, but the family didn't even call Anita until the eve of Mike's funeral. She didn't have time to fly into Chicago and say goodbye to her brother and be at his burial. How could I have been so wrong, how could I have so misjudged this family?

After Mike moved from my apartment in March 2002, neither Anita nor I were given any forwarding address. Presumably, this was at Mike's request. The family had cut all connection with Anita the same way they had erased me from their memory because they felt Anita should have done more for Mike. This was nonsense. Anita lived in California, two thousand miles away. She had a full time job, a husband and a ten-year-old son, Brian. There was no way she could have taken Mike into her home, and Mike would not have wanted to live with her. The Schwartzes, the "wonderful, close-knit family" even stopped remembering their brother's grandchildren on birthdays or special occasions. I wasn't aware of this until Anita and I talked at length after Mike died.

Mike lived in his own apartment from March 2002 until January 2006. Ray's daughter, Myra, told Anita that Mike had been getting along on medications, but then, as often happens with the mentally ill, he decided that the medication had too many side effects. He stopped taking his pills. After that, he withdrew from the family. The landlord called Sharon because he didn't receive the January rent. Sharon had a key to Mike's apartment and went to check on him with her daughter.

Before entering, they called the police. Inside, they found Mike's lifeless body. It was a very sad ending to such a troubled life. Too bad nobody cared to tell me. I have Henry's ashes and I would have asked them to bury the ashes with Mike so they could be together again.

After Henry died and Mike finally moved out, it took two years of therapy to get my life back. Mike's death gave rise to a great deal of anger I thought I had put behind me. Anita also was very upset. We both wonder what we could have done to help Mike survive. However, one thing is for certain: neither of us could have lived with him. Some time after his death, his cousin Sharon called me. I vented all my frustration against the Schwartz family on her. She asked me, "Did you know Mike had a gun?" A gun! Where and when did he get a gun? She explained that Mike got a permit and bought the gun soon after his father died. He lived with me for a year and I didn't know he had a gun. That's a scary scenario. I am not sure what I would have done had I known Mike had a gun while he lived under my roof.

Sharon told me they found the gun permit and the gun in Mike's apartment. She promised to call the following week to make a lunch date. I blurted out my feelings towards this uncaring and unfeeling family. I know I said way too much, but once I started, there was no stopping. I never heard from her again. I suppose there is nothing left to talk about.

In April 2008, Ray died at the age of 84. Nobody informed me. I only found out through an obituary I accidentally read. I wondered whether I should send Ray's wife and children a condolence note. Every once in a while, one of my children repeats something I said many, many years ago. My son Steve reminded me that I taught him that two wrongs never make a right. Evidently some of my teachings when they were little did sink in. I wrote the note, and Faye answered me. However, we've had no further contact.

Anita, her husband Steve and I have kept in touch. They are my children and Tony and Brian are my grandchildren. Because of the miles separating us, I don't know them as well as my other grandchildren. I am happy to have at least a part of Henry with me. It is the summer of 2009. Brian recently graduated high school and Tony is getting married on July 18 in San Francisco. I am looking forward to meeting my new granddaughter-in-law, Alexandra, and seeing Anita's family at the wedding. The last time I saw them was at Henry's funeral in 2001. San Francisco, here I come.

SECTION SIX
MY FRIENDS, MY JEWELS

CHAPTER I
FRIENDS, FRIENDS, WONDERFUL FRIENDS

After we moved to Skokie, I continued my search to find help for Billy. The Jewish Family Service suggested I join a therapy group for recently divorced women. Most of us were in our mid-thirties. At a meeting, I met Ida who became my first friend in the area. Since then, our friendship has endured through bar mitzvahs, weddings and funerals. At the time we met, she too was recently divorced and had problems with her sons adjusting to a single parent home. The big difference between us was that she had loving, supportive parents, while I had no one. During their lifetime, Ida's mom and dad were always very compassionate and kind to my children and me.

In 1981, I married Henry; the following year Ida married Dave. Since then, we have both lost our mates. Over the years, we've continued to laugh and cry together. Our friendship has enriched both our lives and made single parenting a bit easier.

We've talked daily on the telephone for the past 40 plus years. Long ago, we established a routine of having lunch on Saturdays to right the wrongs of the world and catch up on family matters. Recently, Ida's health has been failing, making it difficult for her to get around. I do what I can to make her life easier and keep up her spirits.

I'm always welcome and feel comfortable at the home of Ida's son Joel and his wife Helene. Ida's younger son Lanny and his family live in Omaha.

Some of my other dear friends are survivors. Magda and I are very devoted to the Holocaust Museum. Occasionally, we give joint presentations.

Magda's family has adopted me. I am grateful that they include me in all family functions. I have become Grandma Agnes to Magda's daughter Rochelle, her husband Charlie, their children and grandchildren. Charlie's mother Betty, Grandma Inge, her daughter Sharon, and friends Cheri and Jan are part of this extended family.

Magda and I nursed each other through two serious surgeries. In 2006, I had my right knee replaced. Magda collapsed in my arms in

2008 and had heart valve replacement surgery. We were on our way to hear Eli Wiesel speak at Northwestern University when Magda collapsed in the parking lot in front of her brother and our friend Hilda. Like sisters, we were there to facilitate each other's recovery.

Miklós, Magda's brother, recently moved to Chicago from Cleveland. They now share her home. He is an old-fashioned gentleman who helps ladies put on their coats and opens doors for them. Miklós, better known as Uncle Mike, is a walking encyclopedia. Whether you need information regarding a sporting event or world history, Miklós has the answer at his fingertips.

"Szervusz" in Hungarian is like "Shalom" is in Hebrew. It can be either "hello" or "good-bye." I am a proud member of the Szervusz Club.

Shortly after I married Henry, he took me to Tibor's, a furrier on Dempster in Skokie, to buy me a mink coat. "Tibor" is a typical Hungarian name. I introduced myself and told him I was born in Budapest. As soon as he heard I was of Hungarian descent, he called his sister Ágnes to come and meet me. Ágnes worked next door in a deli. As we chatted, she told me about a group of Hungarian Holocaust survivors who held monthly meetings at each other's homes. They called themselves the Szervusz Club. She took my phone number and told me she would call the next time they met at her house.

After I came to the United States, I had never had any Hungarian friends. I had purposely stayed away from anything Holocaust related. I didn't want to hear about the Holocaust. I didn't want to read about the Holocaust. I didn't want to talk about the Holocaust. I didn't want to remember.

Ágnes kept her word. She called and invited me to a meeting. At first, I was reluctant to go and I made a lame excuse, "I am sorry. I am busy that evening." She was persistent and the next time she called, I accepted her invitation. It was one of the best things I ever did. I met some fantastic ladies who later became dear friends. There are eight "girls" in the group. Originally, we met monthly, but as we grew older, it became more difficult. Now we get together whenever we are able. There are two ladies named Ágnes, two Magdas (one passed away), two

Veras and two Évas (one is Ava). We either have coffee and dessert or lunch at each other's homes. My friend Hilda came to the last meeting and I hope she will remain part of this warm, congenial group. Some of us have lost our husbands. Widowhood has made some friendships stronger. My knowledge of my mother tongue had deteriorated since I only had one long-time friend, Elizabeth, who spoke Hungarian. I speak it much more fluently since I've become part of the "Szervusz Club." While English comes easier to most of us, we end up mixing the two languages. After each meeting, we vow that we will not talk about the Holocaust again, but the subject just refuses to go away. It recurs whenever we are together. It left an indelible mark on all of our lives.

Except for Eva, the rest of us have missed out on a college education. But, we have all rebuilt our lives, carved out careers and raised families. Each one of us is a success story despite the tragedies we suffered early in life.

That mink coat was surely a good buy. It has kept me warm for over twenty-five years, while the friendships it inadvertently created will last forever. Like fine wine and good cheese, our friendships have improved with age. The girls of the Szervusz Club are very special and play an important role in my life.

CHAPTER II
FRIENDS ACROSS THE OCEAN

Every year, through an organization called Action Reconciliation Service for Peace, a young man or woman volunteers to come from Germany to be an intern at the Holocaust Museum in Skokie. My friend Magda lived across the street from the old museum on Main Street and told me about Gregor, an intern she met. She was unbelievably friendly towards him. Not only did she often invite him for lunch, but even offered him a room to spend the night in inclement weather. I said, "What's the matter with you? You're sleeping with the enemy!"

As I got to know Gregor, I realized that he is a sincere, caring young man dedicated to erasing prejudice and genocide and making the world a better place for all mankind. Eventually, I met his parents and his sister. They are also fine people. His oma (grandma) shows her appreciation to Magda and me for having looked after Gregor while in the U.S.A. by keeping in touch with us and sending us wonderful gifts. Her packages are wrapped with great care in a most artistic way. Magda and I have received, among other things, cookies, candy, latte, homemade preserves, embroidered handkerchiefs and towels and other trinkets.

I have often asked myself, "Me, make friends with a German family? Could I really forgive the past?" No, I can't, but I realize these people played no part in the Nazi era. In fact, they are atoning for the sins of their country during World War II. It is time to stop hating, but forgetting is impossible.

After he finished his internship at the museum, Gregor returned to Germany where he attends the University of Ehrfurt. He recently completed a semester of studies in Seoul, Korea. With the wonders of modern technology, we keep in touch. I even helped him edit a couple of school papers via email, from Seoul to Skokie and back.

Then I met Tobias, the intern who followed Gregor. The two young men have very different personalities, but they have a mutual desire to make this world a better place. Tobias, an only child, is a serious violin player. He took me to concerts at Orchestra Hall and at Ravinia.

When his parents came to visit the U.S.A., Magda and I also had the pleasure of meeting them. We found them to be very kind, congenial people. Magda and I refer to the two boys as our adopted grandchildren. When I first met Tobias, his ambition was to become an airline pilot. I suggested he finish his studies first. Then, if he still wanted to be a pilot, he could train for it. I think Tobias has now scrubbed his plans to fly airplanes. He is studying economics at a university in Austria and plans to go to graduate school perhaps in the United States.

Bettina was the intern last year. She was here during the chaotic time when the old small museum was closing and the new and much larger Holocaust Museum and Education Center in Skokie readied for its grand opening in April 2009. I never got to know her as well as her two predecessors. Her internship came to an end in August when she returned to her family and boyfriend in Germany. When Bettina came to the United States, she was already out of college and worked with a theater production group in Germany.

For the opening of the new museum, the German Consul arranged to bring all the former interns to the USA. It was a grand reunion for those who knew all ten. Magda housed our two boys. They had a very hectic but most enjoyable week with us and other friends. Saying good-bye was difficult, so we just said, *Auf weidersehen,* till we meet again.

SECTION SEVEN
TYING UP LOOSE ENDS

CHAPTER I
THE TWILIGHT ZONE

It is 2009. I turned 76 this summer; I am in the twilight of my life. In spite of its ups and downs, life has been a wonderful voyage. I love my little family unconditionally and with all my heart. They made this twisted journey called "life" worthwhile. With them, I have everything. Without them, I have nothing. After many chaotic years, I am now at peace. I am grateful for being relatively healthy. It has become harder to travel, but with advancing years, that's to be expected. I can still walk around the block and get behind the wheel of my car to go wherever I please. Some of my friends are not well enough to care for themselves and require health-care givers. That's a very scary and expensive possibility. I try to help. I'd much rather be the giver than the taker. Several friends are suffering through chemotherapy to treat their cancer, still a truly frightening disease. My children know that I don't want to live on life support or in great pain. I've urged them not to hesitate to pull the plug if my situation becomes hopeless. I don't want to live as a vegetable.

I look in delight at the accomplishments of my children and grandchildren. Hopefully, I will get to see my great-grandchild's beautiful little face soon. I have tried to pass on to my children some of the lessons life taught me. My former co-worker and dear friend Jean used to recite a little ditty: "Love many, trust few, always paddle your own canoe." These few words hold a great deal of truth.

CHAPTER II
MY SECOND CAREER

I have embarked on a second career. Over the years, I had written many stories in my mind, but never put them on paper. In May 1999, Yugoslavia made headline news. I was very upset by Milosevic's ethnic cleansing and started comparing it to the Holocaust. It infuriated me that the world hasn't learned and history was repeating itself. I started writing about my feelings. My writing improved as my anger grew. I decided to submit it to the *Chicago Jewish News* and the *Chicago Sun Times.* They both published my article. The JUF magazine published an abridged version. Since that time, I've written several articles that have been published in various newspapers. My friend Vera presented me with a framed copy of the article that appeared in the Chicago Sun Times. While it has yellowed with age, it still proudly hangs on the wall in my office. Vera's gift was the beginning of a strong, lasting friendship. I also joined Grassfield Writers' Collective, headed by my friend Éva Gross. My short stories have appeared in three of their anthologies. The publication of this biography is partially financed by a grant from Niles Township.

In 2003, on my friend Mary's recommendation, I became editor of the Skokie Art Guild's monthly newsletter. I love this job and I make a few dollars doing something I enjoy. The Guild is made up of warm and friendly people and I've made new friends. I've also learned new computer skills. My curiosity about the computer reaches beyond creating a document. I want to know why and how it works.

My doctor recently asked me, "What do you do for exercise?"

I told him, "I sit in front of the computer and my fingers dance on the keyboard." I don't think that's the answer he wanted.

For over fifty years, I was silent about the Holocaust. Now I am speaking up. I feel it incumbent upon me to tell my story to young people. My drawers bulge with "fan mail" received from the multitude of children who have listened to my story. It is a difficult story to tell, but it must be told so the younger generation will remember they met a Holocaust survivor. My aim is to honor those who perished by preventing the Holocaust from becoming just another page in a history book. As a member of the Speakers Bureau of the Illinois Holocaust Museum and Education Center, I reach a variety of young people. Busloads of youngsters come to the museum to hear me talk about the past. I also travel and make presentations at outlying schools. Usually, my audience consists of eighth graders. However, I have also spoken to younger children as well as adults. The intelligent questions they ask are very gratifying. It means they listened and heard what I had to say. I always emphasize their good fortune of living in a free country. Children today don't appreciate living in a democracy. They don't know what life is under tyranny. They were born in the Land of the Free.

My son Billy accompanied me to a radio interview. He now refers to me as a "freelance writer and public speaker." I appreciate my new title.

CHAPTER III
HITLER'S LEGACY

By now, I have heard many survivors tell their sad stories. Each story is different, yet the same. The common denominator is TRAGEDY. We have all suffered a great tragedy because of Hitler's Final Solution. This baggage stays with us forever. Many of our subsequent decisions grew out of the tragedy that befell us. Most of us have rebuilt our lives and have gone forward, but the loss we suffered as a result of the Nazi era has changed our lives permanently. Important decisions I've made as a result of the Holocaust have also affected my children's and my grandchildren's lives.

Hitler blamed everything on the Jews and I blame Hitler and his followers for everything that happened to the Jews during his era. I personally blame him for ruining my life by taking my mother away from me. Jews have a history of being peace-loving, educated people. Who knows how many budding scientists the Nazis killed who might have found cures for terrible illnesses?

For many post-war years, I had a "Hitler mentality." I never denied that I was Jewish, but I never allowed my children to wear any religious jewelry. I strongly felt that our religion was nobody's business. I was scared to be a Jew and I raised my family accordingly. I felt it was more important to assimilate than to be Jewish. On Jewish holidays, or at any Jewish gathering, I still fear that someone will throw a hand grenade or a bomb into the crowd. The recent shooting at the Washington D.C. Holocaust Museum reinforced this fear.

I am the least religious among my survivor friends. At times I still question, "How could an ever-loving God allow the murder of six million Jews? Where was He while the ovens of Auschwitz burned night and day?" These are theological questions that people much smarter than I am have not been able to answer.

I do regret not teaching my children more about our rich heritage. I have no doubt that my grandchildren will intermarry. They have grown up in a Gentile world. Sometimes I ask myself, "Will my grandchildren be better off having totally assimilated?" And then I think of my Orthodox grandparents. "Did they die because of their faith?" Of course, when Hitler's henchmen murdered them, they didn't care whether they were religious or not. They were just "dirty Jews."

I have great respect and love for my fellow Jews and Israel; I support them in any way I can. It is organized religion that doesn't appeal to me and actually scares me. I find religious fanatics of every faith frightening. People with faith weather the storms of life more easily. They are able to turn overwhelming problems over to God. I can't do that; I don't have that kind of faith.

How many generations will it take for that snowball to stop rolling?

CHAPTER IV
AFTERTHOUGHTS

I look at my three middle-aged children and wonder why they are all single. This is not what I hoped for them. I wanted them to find loving lifetime mates. I would rest easier knowing that each has a partner and knows reciprocal love and caring. My eldest never married. He was engaged once, but the engagement was broken. I have asked myself many times, "Was he scared of marriage because of the loss of his father and the heartache he watched me endure as a child growing up?"

Billy my middle child, missed his father the most. His teenage problems emanated from a longing for his father. They were very close. Today at least, he has a son who loves him, but that's not the same as a lifetime partner. He had a brief bad marriage and I understand why it didn't last, but he was very young when that marriage ended. Why hasn't he remarried? His primary goal was to raise his only child. Now his son Charles is grown and has a family of his own, albeit, 2,000 miles away. Why don't my boys desire the intimacy of love? Perhaps they seek independence and don't want to be reliant on anybody. Is this the lifestyle of my children's generation? To me loving someone and being loved has always been important.

During her teens my daughter was cheated out of the adoration of a loving father. Fathers play important roles in the lives of teenage daughters. Could the lack of a father in her life be the reason she got restless and wanted a divorce after ten years of marriage? She has three grown children who are now scattered and leading their own lives. Her boyfriend Jim and his family stand by her side and I appreciate that they have taken her into their hearts. It would give me comfort to know that she is married, but today's society does not live by the old rules. My children don't appear to be unhappy with their single status and I can't live their lives. My parents were happily married and so were Aunt Betsy and Uncle Eugene. I grew up seeing happy family lives. Did my sad marriage influence my children so much that they prefer living without a mate or is it perhaps just a sign of the times?

Adolf Hitler, if you didn't destroy my family, would my children's lives be better today?

Without a doubt.

There goes that snowball again tumbling down the hill, picking up more snow as it rolls along.

CHAPTER V
EPILOGUE

I never thought I would see so much uncertainty again in my life. The great oceans that surround our country have for centuries given Americans a feeling of complacency. Until the attack of September 11, Americans have rarely seen war on their soil. This attack proved that we have lived with a false sense of security. Our enemies didn't need sophisticated weaponry to create chaos and the loss of many lives.

Our elected officials undermined our great nation's Constitution. In the name of protection from unknown enemies, the administration bent the rules and we have lost a multitude of civil rights. I feel violated by cameras on street corners monitoring scofflaws. Cameras, wiretapping, where does it stop? Big brother is everywhere looking over our shoulders. They even intrude into our bedrooms. The ideals that created this great nation are being trampled upon. Prisoners held without specific charges and the lack of speedy trials don't sit well with me.

Immigrants settled and built our great Country as they looked for freedom and an open society. I realize we have a multitude of modern enemies who put no value on their own lives. How do we cope with them without violating our Constitution? I am not sure anyone has a viable answer.

I never thought that we would see the Great Depression return. We seem to be on the verge of it. What happened to the growing economy throughout the world? The standard of living improved with each generation. Now we are moving backwards. Retirement savings have been wiped out. Jobs have been lost in virtually every field. I am concerned for the next generation. What kind of debt will they inherit and how will it affect their lives? Will the same social benefits I am receiving, such as Medicare and Social Security, be available to them?

My children constantly tell me that I am a pessimist. My cup is always half empty rather than half full. They are probably right. Our lives shape our outlook. My life has been built on tragedy and sorrow, but I hope the cups of my children and grandchildren will overflow with good health, joy and happiness.

Despite our many problems, I am convinced that the United Sates is still the best place to live in the world. I have confidence that the pendulum will again swing the other way and there will be peace and prosperity. That's the kind of world I wish to leave for my children, grandchildren and all their descendants.

My concerns reach out to Israel where so many Jews have fled to live without persecution in a country of their own. The elderly Israelis have lived through Hitler's Final Solution and their battered bodies and souls found freedom in a new land. The younger generations sacrifice their lives to build and maintain a land of their own. Israelis live much more difficult lives than Americans. Their belief in Israel keeps them there despite frequent terrorist attacks. The Arab world wants to push tiny little Israel into the sea. The United States, its only ally, must not allow the destruction of Israel, the only democracy in the Middle East.

NEVER AGAIN must be taught in the schools and remembered from generation to generation all over the world.

I still envision and hope for a better world.

God bless my family. God bless the U.S.A. God bless Israel.

Would you like to see your manuscript become a book?

**If you are interested in becoming a
PublishAmerica author, please submit your
manuscript for possible publication to us at:**

acquisitions@publishamerica.com

You may also mail in your manuscript to:

**PublishAmerica
PO Box 151
Frederick, MD 21705**

www.publishamerica.com

CPSIA information can be obtained at www.ICGtesting.com
Printed in the USA
LVOW040317141011

250423LV00002B/14/P